Praise for The 10-Minute Refresh for Moms

If you are a busy mom who feels pulled in a million directions, overwhelmed, and in total need of a recharge, you definitely want to read *The 10-Minute Refresh for Moms!* As a mom and professional myself, I know I just love the encouragement, empowerment, and practical strategies Nichole Clark offers in this book. Nichole writes in a way that makes you feel like you're sitting across the table with her having a heart-to-heart chat. She is authentic and humorous, and she makes you realize how much you deserve to take care of yourself. She offers simple and quick strategies to integrate self-care, self-compassion, and kindness into your daily life so that you can feel good and do good in the world. She also shows you how to bring your children and family into these practices and how to be the role model for who you want your children to be. This is a must-read for busy moms everywhere!

—Dr. Colleen Georges, TEDx Speaker, Coach, & Author of *RESCRIPT the Story You're Telling Yourself*

Nichole Clark invites you in like an old friend and reminds you of the little things that matter most. I couldn't get her chapter on gratitude out of my mind for days. Waking up with gratitude had always been something I tried to do, but I must have lost the habit somewhere along the way. Thank you, Nichole, for bringing back a piece of my heart.

—Nanette O'Neal, author of *A Doorway Back to Forever: BELIEVE, A Doorway Back to Forever: TRUST, and A Doorway Back to Forever: DEFEND*

"I love how refreshing this book is to my soul. I love Nichole's realness and life stories. It's an easy read for busy moms. She shares her own life experiences and struggles which makes it really easy for anyone to connect with her because the stories she shares are areas we all struggle with and need to grow in, like loving ourselves better. If you are a mom or busy woman looking to learn how to improve your self- esteem and grow in confidence this is the book for you!"
—Dana Lyons, Founder of *ALL ONE Ministries* and author of *No Longer Cinderella*

When I met Nichole, there was an instant connection. Maybe it was the mom connection, maybe the curlfriend connection? Either way, I knew I'd met a woman to admire. She is a champion for moms, for women really. Even though we are in different places as moms, I'm an empty-nester and she just had number six, the habits she shares apply! Nichole's book *The 10-Minute Refresh for Moms*, teaches simple yet practical steps that can transform your daily life and the impact you have on your children.
—Brenda A. Haire, author of *Save the Butter Tubs! Discover Your Worth in a Disposable World*

GRAB YOUR FREE GIFT!

Download the Companion Workbook

(Retails for $39.95... Yours FREE!)

Each chapter in this book ends with a section called, "Actions to Take." This companion workbook will take those actions a step deeper and give you more clarity and support on your transformational journey.

While reading a book can certainly help you, *applying* the things you learn will make the most difference in your life. I highly recommend *actively* utilizing the tools in this workbook and book, if you want to see a change for the better.

You should download the workbook for this edition right now, so you can work along as you read. To access your gift:

1. Go to go.refreshformoms.com/gift.
2. Tell us where to email the access link.
3. Check your email, then download the PDF.
4. Have fun following along as you read the book.

THE 10-MINUTE REFRESH FOR MOMS:

Less Stress, More Joy

NICHOLE B. CLARK

Hardback: 978-1-64085-484-0
Paperback: 978-1-64085-483-3

TABLE OF CONTENTS

Note to Reader   xi

Introduction: It's Only a Matter of Time   xiii

1. Habit One: The Single Most Powerful Thing You
   Can Do To Instantly Improve Your Life   1

    a. The Bookends of Your Day   3
    b. The Definition of Gratitude   4
    c. Your Altitude   6
    d. There is Always Something to Be
       Grateful For   8
    e. Gratitude Journal   10
    f. Little Black Book   12
    g. The Grateful Game   15

2. Habit Two: Learn to Relax   20

    a. Being a Mom is Super Stressful   21
    b. Side Effects of Stress   22
    c. Using Stress to Our Advantage   26
    d. Being Mindful   26

    e. Slow Down and Take a Breather   29
    f. How to Deep Breathe   30
    g. Benefits of Deep Breathing   31

3. Habit Three: Enjoy the Natural Things in Life   36
    a. Take a Ten-Minute Nature Walk   37
    b. Observe Animals   38
    c. Sacred Reflections   40
    d. Hard Lessons   41
    e. Facebook   43
    f. Abundance & Benefits   44
    g. Frequently Visit the Fountain of Life:
       Stay Hydrated   45
    h. What Do You Drink the Most?   47
    i. Sugary Drinks and Our Health   48

4. Habit Four: Replace Criticism & Comparisons
   with Compliments   54
    a. Who is Your Very Worst Enemy?   55
    b. The Real Enemy   58
    c. Awaken the Cheerleader   59
    d. Recognizing the Enemy Within   60
    e. I Hate My Body   62
    f. Do You Measure Up?   63
    g. Retraining the Needy Critic   64
    h. Learn How to Accept a Compliment   67
    i. Give Compliments   69

5. Habit Five: Change Your Words   74
    a. The Power of Words   75
    b. What Labels Do You Have?   77
    c. Changing the Vocabulary We Use   79
    d. Four 4-Letter Words   80
    e. Spy on Yourself and Take Notes   83

f.   Just Say, "No!"   84
g.   Just Say, "Please?"   87
h.   What Do You Expect?   89
i.   Let Go   91
j.   Lower Your Expectations   93
k.   Do You Have the Bad Habit
     of Complaining?   96

6. Habit Six: Start Seeing Yourself for
    Who You Really Are   103

    a.   Mirror Work   104
    b.   You Are Enough   105
    c.   What is an Affirmation?   108
    d.   How to Write an Affirmation   112
    e.   Keep it Positive   113
    f.   Set Your Day up for Success   116

7. Habit Seven: Get Enough Quality Sleep   121

    a.   Do You Get Enough ZZZs?   122
    b.   Take Naps When You Can   123
    c.   What is Your Sleep Number?   124
    d.   The Facts About Sleep   125
    e.   How to Lull Yourself to Sleep   127
    f.   You Can Retrain Your Brain
         While You Sleep   129

8. Habit Eight: Feel Good Now-
    The Power of Visualization   133

    a.   My Wake-up Call   134
    b.   Dream Document   136
    c.   How to Be Like a Child Again   139
    d.   The Ones That "Make it"   140
    e.   What do *You* Want?   142
    f.   Find Your Why   143

9. Habit Nine: Set Goals that Scare You &
    Share Your Masterpiece   151

    a. Set Goals   152
    b. Don't Give up Before You Even Start   154
    c. Pushups Challenge   156
    d. Got 4-Minutes?   161
    e. Celebrating the Little Things   162
    f. What Will Your Masterpiece Be?   165
    g. Magical Mornings   166
    h. What if You Fail?   169
    i. YOU-nique   171
    j. Don't Die with Your Music Still in You   173
    k. To Fly Means to Truly Live   175

10. Habit Ten: Don't Worry, Be Happy   183

    a. Are You a Chronic Worrier?   184
    b. We Are Like Magnets   186
    c. Don't Worry, Be Happy   189
    d. How to Stop Worrying   190
    e. The Bright Side or the Brown Side   192
    f. The Dream That Woke Me Up   194
    g. What Makes You Smile?   198
    h. Laughter Is the Best Medicine   202

Conclusion   209
Want Help Applying What You've Learned?   217
Acknowledgements   219
Dedication to my Dad   221
References   223

NOTE TO READER

I have written this book for busy moms who feel like they never have enough time for themselves. I want to reassure you that where there is a will, there is a way. You have time for what you make time for, and you make time for the things that you *want*. It's all about priorities. Ten minutes is all that I'm asking of you. Your sanity, health, and happiness are important to me, and more importantly, your family. I designed this book to be an easy read that will quickly allow you to make small yet profound changes in your life to yield instant happiness and hope.

In mere minutes you can feel refreshed and capable of handling whatever comes your way. This book is filled with simple steps that will allow you to see how easy it can be to fit self-care into your life. Please do not underestimate the power of the little things and of filling your own cup.

So many mothers I know pour into others all day long. They give time and energy to their kids, their husband, their jobs, friends, even strangers; but so often put themselves on the back burner. Things can only stay on the back burner for so long before they either become cold and stale or they go up in flames. Please don't allow that to happen to you. It is so much easier to fill the "cups" of others, when our own is full. Instead of emptying ourselves each time we help others, we can become so filled up that our excess pours over onto them and leaves all involved feeling good.

You are not alone. You are loved, valued, and needed. Please don't feel guilty for taking a few moments of your day for yourself. I promise that by taking some time to recharge your own battery and put yourself first, you are not being selfish, you are setting the best example for your kids that you can. Your family wants a happy, healthy, fun mom. They don't want you to feel stressed, worried, or overwhelmed. I'm sure you want the same things.

The tips in this book will each take you no longer than ten minutes to do. No matter how busy you are, you can find ten minutes!

I truly believe that the hand that rocks the cradle has one of the most impactful roles in the world. If the mom behind that hand does not have energy to take care of her body, does not like herself, believe in herself, or pursue goals, her children will follow suit. Are you ready to put yourself first and feel hope that you won't be stuck with mom guilt forever? Are you ready to make yourself a priority *for your sanity, your family, and the world*? Let's discover how that is possible in just ten minutes of your day! Let's do this!

*Disclaimer: I was raised with a Christian background and make a few references to the Higher Power in which I believe throughout the book. When I refer to God, the Spirit, or the Lord please interject your own personal belief system (ie: The Universe, your Higher Power, the Energy Field, Karma, etc). Know that no matter what you believe, there is a higher power out there that loves you completely exactly the way you are and wants you to feel immensely happy.

INTRODUCTION
IT'S ONLY A MATTER OF TIME

"Happiness is not a checklist. A dream job, a fast car, a good home, even love, mean nothing at all if you have not yet found a way to feel full and content in your own mind and heart."
—Beau Taplin

"You will never find time for anything. If you want time, you must make it."
—Charles Brixton

I'll be Happy When...

Have you ever found yourself saying "I'll be happy when _____?"

I know I have. Here are a few examples of what I thought would bring me happiness:

"I'll be happy when I hit my goal weight." "When I finally own a house." "When the house is paid off." "When I don't have to change diapers anymore." "When I get a good nights' sleep." "When my husband/I retire(s)." Etc. Etc. I could go on and on. I used that phrase for years as an excuse to why I wasn't happy.

I can't even count how many times I have said that phrase, or something similar over my lifetime. It seems I was always looking forward to something in the future rather than being content with the present.

I have been married for 16 years. We are expecting our sixth child soon, have lived in four states, nine different apartments and homes, and have accrued a lifetime worth of experiences and adventures since we tied the knot.

My children are between the ages of seven and fifteen (minus the one in utero) and there are so many things I wish I could go back and tell my younger self.

As a young mother, the days were so jumbled and mixed up it seemed I never knew the time of day or day of the week. I was frazzled, tired, and the epitome of a "hot mess." I longed for the day that I could take a shower by myself, go to the bathroom without someone watching or screaming outside the door, or take a simple nap.

I spent the majority of my time cleaning up after kids (only to have the rest of the house destroyed as I cleaned one room); changing diapers (only to turn around and do it again within the hour); or trying to take care of every need, whimper, or whine from my kids. When it came to "me" time it seemed that all I wanted to do was sleep.

I'm not kidding.

I remember my husband asking me one day, "If you could go anywhere in the world, where would you go?" You know what I said? "To bed."

He rolled his eyes and clearly didn't seem to appreciate how very exhausted and worn out I was.

I lived my life on auto-pilot and all the days seemed to mesh together with our routine of waking up, eating breakfast, cleaning the house, watching Dora or some other lame cartoon that numbed my brain (but kept the kids entertained). I'd play with the kids, eat lunch, and then indulge in my beloved nap time. I have always been a stickler for naps. Sometimes I found that I was more anxious to sleep than my kiddos, yet religiously gave myself as much time to rest as I could. My afternoons were pretty much a repeat of my mornings, except that I had to fit making dinner in there as well as getting myself somewhat presentable for my husband and making the house look like I'd actually done something all day. Yep, I'd wait until right before he came home to get ready for the day, because otherwise my makeup would be melted, my shirt covered in stains, and my hair might as well stay in my mom-bun. In all honesty, I probably greeted him without "getting ready" more often than not.

Every day seemed the same and every day I wished that I could find "joy" in the journey.

Rather than finding bliss among the skinned knees and spilled milk, more often than not I found myself longing for the day that I didn't have to bring a diaper bag or use a car seat everywhere I went. I yearned for the freedom that I had lost and to feel like myself again.

I love my kids to pieces and wouldn't change my situation for the world. In fact, I feel extremely blessed to have been able to have them all easily and to stay at home with them.

However, with my husband gone more often than not, and not owning a second vehicle, I found myself feeling lonely, overwhelmed, and lost. It wasn't that I was unhappy, but looking back, I certainly wasn't happy. I was somewhere in between. There were short blissful moments of intense happiness and joy scattered among long, drawn-out weeks of pure chaos and fatigue.

I often found myself thinking and believing that someday I would be "happy" again and find time for me.

I was right. Now that my kids are older and "easier" to take care of (at least physically), I have a lot more time for myself. I love my current life situation and have been able to reinvent myself in such a way that every day seems like a joyful dream.

However, I could've had this kind of joy and happiness all along the way, had I known some simple, yet life-changing tips that I will be sharing in this book. These are the things that I wish I could go back and tell my younger, frazzled self to save my sanity and make motherhood full of joy.

The first thing I have learned has to do with time. As a twenty-something mom with five little ones between the ages of 0-7, I felt like I never had any time. I didn't have time to exercise, to eat right, to read, write, or play the piano. I could barely find the time to shower, so how could I possibly find the time for self-love or improvement?

Let's talk about time for a minute.

How Much Time Do We Need?

Time is a bit of a funny thing. We all say that we don't have time for certain things, but really, we have time for what we make time for. It is a matter of prioritization and putting first things first. We all have the same 24 hours in a day, yet how every single person uses them is as different as the sands of the sea. Some of us waste a lot of time and some of us work non-stop and have no balance.

When I think back upon the way I spent my time as a young mother, I see some gaps and holes that I was filling with the wrong things. Because I had no energy by the time the kids went to bed, I spent nearly every evening either watching a movie or scrolling Facebook trying to feel connected to other adults until I'd fall asleep. I often didn't get to see my husband (who was in medical school at the time) until late at night when I was ready for bed. I made up excuse after excuse as to why I couldn't do the things that I knew I was supposed to do. In reality, I was wasting a lot of precious time in front of a screen or device, trying to feel "connected."

Sometimes I felt like my life resembled the movie *Groundhog Day*[1]. I'd wake up and repeat the exact same steps as yesterday, with little variation and not much exhilaration.

Let's fast forward to a night a few years ago, when my daughter and I made a simple, yet significant, discovery that changed my life.

My then eight-year-old daughter complained about doing the dishes, which was typical. Try as I might I could not get her to see the light. No amount of sympathy, lecturing, or explanation could get her to comprehend that I wasn't an evil witch.

She believed that the dishes would take her all night and that I was her mortal enemy. In reality, she spent far more time crying and whining about the job than what it'd take to just do it.

I decided to play a little game of math with her, to show her that I really wasn't asking too much. We started calculating how much time out of her day it took her to do the dishes. We decided that we each needed a bare minimum of six hours of sleep. That left us with eighteen hours to do what we wanted during the day. Since there are sixty minutes in an hour, we multiplied 18x60. That gave us 1,080 minutes of awake time a day.

We then decided to time how long it took her to do the dishes, which was roughly around ten minutes. If you take 1,080 and multiply it by 0.1 (ten percent) you get 108 minutes. So, 108 minutes= 10% of our awake time in a day. Take ten percent of that, and you get 10.8 minutes. That means that less than 11 minutes in a day is *one percent* of our day.

When I asked my daughter if she could handle helping out around the house for 1% of her day, she understood that I really wasn't asking too much of her after all. It was like giving me a penny for every dollar she had. No big deal.

From that moment on, I have been able to use the same logic on myself.

Instead of complaining or feeling like the laundry, cleaning, and cooking were taking up my entire day, I started to time myself. I began playing the game of "racing the clock" and trying to beat my last time of getting a certain job done.

Within days I found that I had a lot more time than I thought. I learned that the "chores" of motherhood were not all that bad and didn't take as much time as I believed. In fact, the more that I beat the clock, the more time I had to do the things that I loved and enjoyed. I could fit time in to play with my kids or read a good book. I found more joy and bliss and learned several things that I could do in one percent of my time that made all the difference in my happiness.

I had wasted *way more* than ten minutes of my time scrolling social media or doing mindless activities, when I could've been doing something that contributed to my feeling good about myself. Falling into the traps of mindlessly watching TV, playing Cookie Jam, or comparing myself to others on my phone were bad habits that were robbing me of my joy and my time. It wasn't my kids' fault that I was miserable; it was my own.

I often felt sick and tired, struggled with low self-worth and body image, and felt like a failure. I knew that something needed to change.

I knew that my four daughters and son were always watching me and were learning from my poor example. It dawned on me that if I didn't change my opinion of myself or the way I spent my time, I would be teaching them to do the very same things. I had no intention of raising children that had no self-esteem or that felt unworthy of taking the time to take care of themselves.

The pain of seeing what I was doing to them, or would do if I didn't change, was enough to make me want to change. I was determined to choose to improve myself every day until I became the kind of person I wanted my children to become. Being selfish for the first time in years finally felt like a good thing rather than a huge sin.

I decided that I was worth *at a very minimum* one percent of my day. In fact, the more time I took for myself, the more that percentage of time increased and the more time I found for me. As a result, in a very short amount of time, I became the kind of person I want my kids to be (most of the time- nobody's perfect). I found that if I focused on me, they naturally wanted to follow in my footsteps, and for once that was okay with me.

I am asking you the same thing: *Are you worth one percent of your time? What about ten percent? Are you willing to be "selfish" enough to take ten minutes or more daily to improve yourself, feel refreshed, and find your joy? Are you ready to become the kind of person you want your children to become? Do you want to love yourself and your life?*

If you are like me and care about the example you set for your children, I have written this book for you. If you want to feel good about yourself and the time you have with your little ones, this book is for you. If you want to find fast, free, and fun life hacks that make you come alive and feel both happy and healthy, this book is for you. I have filled it with super simple yet life-changing habits that you can easily fit into your day without much effort.

There are ten main things that I have found to make a profound impact on my happiness and my life. The more I practice them, the more I wish I would've known about them fifteen years ago when I began my journey through motherhood. Each of these habits is effective and takes as little as one percent of your day. Are you ready to learn what they are?

HABIT ONE:
THE SINGLE MOST POWERFUL THING YOU CAN DO TO INSTANTLY IMPROVE YOUR LIFE

"Be thankful for what you have, you'll end up having more. If you concentrate on what you don't have, you will never, ever have enough."
—Oprah Winfrey

"In ordinary life, we hardly realize that we receive a great deal more than we give, and that it is only with gratitude that life becomes rich."
—Dietrich Bonhoeffer

If I told you there was one single habit that would do more for your overall well-being and happiness than any other thing, in only a few minutes a day, what would you think it is?

Let me list a few of the scientifically proven benefits of this practice, to see if you can guess it:

- Makes you happier
- Improves physical and psychological health by reducing stress and toxic emotions
- Helps your relationships: deepens existing relationships and brings more friends into your life
- Makes people like you more
- Helps you sleep better and feel better
- Increases your self-esteem
- Improves mental strength and helps you overcome trauma
- Proven to have long lasting positive effects on the brain
- Increases productivity and energy
- Makes you more likely to exercise
- Improves decision making and goal achievement
- Helps you live longer
- Makes you more optimistic
- Boosts your career[2]

Can you guess what it is yet? I'll give you a hint, it rhymes with attitude and helps improve it too! Yep, it is the practice of gratitude.

Before researching for this book, I knew that gratitude was important, and I loved the way that being grateful made me *feel*, but I honestly had no idea how good it was for me. If there is anything you can take away from reading this book at all, **this is the number one thing**. It is so simple you can do it any time anywhere, yet it is the most powerful thing you can get into the habit of doing.

It takes seconds of time to think of something to be grateful for. That means that it doesn't even take one percent of your day to improve everything about your life. In fact, when you do the math, it is more like $1/1000^{th}$ of your day. I'd say there are no excuses for not being able to fit this into your life.

By developing a daily habit of being grateful, you can actually start and end your day on a good note. I have been practicing the following routine for years now and it has done wonders for my mental sanity and for handling my kids with more kindness and patience.

The Bookends of Your Day

No matter what time of day, or where you are, gratitude can soothe your soul and make you feel great in an instant. At a minimum, we should start and end our day with gratitude (hence the bookends). There is something magical about writing, thinking, or saying out loud the things we are grateful for. It changes our mood and helps us look for the good in our lives and not the bad.

Expressing gratitude is as simple as finding something good to say/feel about the things or experiences we have in our lives. By looking for the things that bring us joy, we soon find that there is an endless array of things to be grateful for.

Every day when I wake up, I immediately find a few reasons to be grateful and I think about them. I do this even before I get out of bed. Immediately upon hearing my alarm, I press snooze and use those seven minutes of my day to first think of at least ten reasons

I feel grateful, then to plan my day in my mind so that it goes well.

When I start my day by thinking of something to be grateful for, I feel blessed and happy. It is as easy as thinking, "Thank you for another day to be alive." Or "I'm grateful I woke up, I know some people aren't going to today." Or, "I'm so thankful for a great night's sleep."

It starts me off on the right track. When we think about things that make us happy, we feel happy. There is a universal law that says what we focus on expands. When we focus on the things that we are grateful for, we will attract more things for which to be grateful.

You can give thanks for a good night's sleep, or for the fact that you have a bed to sleep in (even if it wasn't the best night's sleep). It doesn't matter how small or trivial the blessing may seem, expressing gratitude for it will open your eyes to how very good you really have it.

The Definition of Gratitude

The dictionary defines gratitude as "the quality of feeling or being grateful or thankful".[3] When we express gratitude, it is as much about the *feeling* behind it as it is the words that we are saying. We can all say, "thank you" and not mean it. We can say it sarcastically or with no feeling whatsoever. It is important to *really feel grateful* rather than going through the motions. I tell my kids when we are praying that it is not about what you say as much as how you *feel* about what you are saying.

Many people never even say the words and don't really feel thankful for what others have done for them, having learned to expect things for nothing. We can help our kids avoid the entitlement plague by simply teaching them this one skill of expressing thanks.

To really live a life with gratitude, we must really *feel* grateful. We must not only express thanks but do so with sincerity and feeling.

People can often tell whether someone is grateful or not and they usually want to give more to those people who express gratitude than to those who do not.

My kids are perfect examples of this. When I want to treat them to something special, like going out to dinner or on a trip, I expect them to not only say *thank you*, but to really show that they do not take these things for granted and notice how blessed they are. Something as simple as giving me a hug, saying "thanks," or writing a nice note encourages me to reward that child even more. On the other hand, when my children act like they "deserve some reward" or as if it is "their right," I struggle to want to give them more. Receiving gratitude from someone else often motivates the giver to give even more things, although that should not be our motivation for giving thanks.

The Bible teaches us this same lesson in the story of the ten lepers who came to Jesus for healing. After telling them to go wash in the river, only one came back to express thanks. Imagine that. Leprosy was the worst plague of the day and having it made you a complete social outcast. No one wanted to be around you if you had such a disease. You would think that after being healed in a very simple and fast way, you would want to express thanks for this miracle. Since nine out of the ten lepers did not do so, we learn that it is not the first inclination of many of us to give thanks where thanks are due.[4]

Apparently the idea of entitlement has existed for a very long time.

I would like to believe that if I were healed from such an appalling disease that robbed me of health, joy, and social interaction, I would be wise enough to give back in praise.

You can't be truly happy if you are not grateful.

Your Altitude

I remember in high school they used to have cheesy motivational posters on the walls. I often like cheesy things. One of my favorites that has stuck with me over the years was a picture of a hot air balloon up in the sky, with the words, "your attitude determines your altitude." Although I've always been afraid of heights and might never go in a hot air balloon, I loved the picture and the message.

Gratitude changes your attitude, and attitude determines your altitude. "Altitude" is a way of determining how "high" you are. If you are happy, you are flying high and feeling good. The higher you are, the happier you are. I am not referring to the "high" one gets from drugs, but from the natural high you can feel by being grateful. People in high school actually used to ask me if I was "high". I'd always say, "Yes! I'm high on life!" (and I have never tried drugs). I truly felt that way back then, and although it left me for most of my adult life, that feeling has returned, and I am overjoyed. I give the majority of the credit of my restored happiness to the developing of the simple habit of gratitude.

No matter how bad you have it, there is guaranteed to be someone out there who has it worse. When you recognize how blessed you are, you become more blessed. It's an amazing concept to grasp.

If you would love to feel "high on life" might I prescribe a daily dose of gratitude? You can do it anywhere at any time. It is a great thing to do when you are stuck behind a slow driver, at a red light, waiting in line, bored during class, etc. This is a practice that will bring so much joy to your life and is so very easy to do. The next time you feel like complaining, replace your complaint with something that makes you feel happy or grateful and you'll soon find you have nothing left to complain about.

For example, when the line at the grocery store is so long that you have to wait a few minutes to check out, rather than fuss and gripe about it, choose to be grateful that you have a store to shop at and money to purchase the things in your cart.

A positive attitude can also affect our health.

Research has proven "those with a positive attitude about aging lived more than seven years longer than those who had a more negative outlook about growing older. Attitude has more of an influence on longevity than blood pressure, cholesterol levels, smoking, body weight, or level of exercise."[5]. Optimists therefore, live longer, and are happier and healthier both physically and mentally.

Learning how to be grateful and express gratitude can change a pessimist to an optimist. Everyone has the power within to make the change to be happier and healthier, just by making the choice to do so.

If you want to feel happy, find something to be grateful for. Identify someone that you appreciate having around and tell them how glad you are to have them in your life. If you can't find anyone to thank for being in your life, find something else—whether it be a part of your body or a physical possession you have, your car, a pet, etc., and express your gratitude for it.

We all have many things to be grateful for, if we become aware of them. When we start looking for and appreciating the little things, we will have a continual flow of more and more good things brought our way.

There is Always Something to Be Grateful For

When you think about the hard things so many people have to go through, most often our trials and problems seem very miniscule. I am a pretty big wimp most of the time, especially when it comes to the cold. I used to complain and whine every time it snowed or got below thirty degrees. However, as I have learned more about the power of positive thinking, even this has improved in my life.

On a recent walk this past winter, I began by thinking how grateful I was that I had a coat to wear and boots to keep my feet warm in the winter snow. I thought about how pretty the snow looked and gave thanks that I could see. I listened to some soothing music while doing so. I felt grateful for sounds and that I had working ears to hear them, and so on and so on. This has since become a daily habit. You see, when you get started, you notice more and more things that are typically taken for granted and you feel more and more grateful.

In *The Power* by Rhonda Byrnes, it states, "Be grateful! Gratitude costs you nothing, but it is worth more than all the riches in the world. Gratitude enriches you with all the riches in life, because whatever you're grateful for multiplies!"[6]

> *"Gratitude is the song of the soul that will lift any individual into joy and light no matter what his condition is."*[7]

> *"Gratitude turns what we have into enough."*
> Anonymous

Do you believe that? I hope so, for in finding something to be grateful for, even in the hardest times, we can find hope and see that our lives get better. As a mother I can readily admit there have been many days that if it weren't for the gift of gratitude, I might have thrown in the towel.

When the kids are fighting and making messes it can be challenging to find something to be grateful for. In those moments, I like to ponder about what life would really be like without them. Sure, I wouldn't have as many messes to clean up or as much stress (at least I like to think that), but I also would have a huge void in my life. My children are some of my most precious blessings and even on the hard days I wouldn't change being a mother to them for the world. It also helps me on those especially hard days to think of times in history when mothers had it much worse than I do, like during World War II. Thinking of and learning about how the people of that time handled the situations presented to them is really inspirational.

In Viktor Frankl's book, *Mans Search for Meaning*[8], he explains how he and the other people in the concentration camps during Hitler's regime had all of their material possessions taken from them. He observed however, that they could not take away his mind or the way he thought or responded to the situation. They could take his books, his clothing, his family and friends, and ration his food, *but they could not take his ability to see things the way he wanted to see them*. He talks about how he dreamed of getting out of the camps and teaching seminars around the world about his concepts of mind over reality. He proved through his own example, that the power of a man's thoughts can get them through the most terrible situations of life.

He says, "...man is ultimately self-determining...In the concentration camps, for example, in this living laboratory and on this testing ground, we watched and witnessed some of our comrades behave like swine while others behaved like saints. Man has both potentialities within himself; which one is actualized depends on decisions but not on conditions... After all, man is that being who invented the gas chambers of Auschwitz; however, he is also that being who entered those gas chambers upright, with the Lord's Prayer or the Shema Yisrael on his lips." He says people can take everything away from us but the way we think and respond to life. He had a grateful heart and a beautiful way of responding to life and making the best out of the awful. He knew how to make the most sour of lemons into delicious lemonade.

If someone like Viktor can have his family, his house, his career, and everything he owned taken from him and still be grateful, how can I possibly complain when my kids make a huge mess or make me lose some sleep? What did the mothers of those days do to stay sane? When I think of all that they had to go through, how could I even think about how hard my life is? I couldn't even compare.

When we choose grateful thoughts rather than unkind or mean thoughts, we open the gates of our minds to take us away from our current realities and experience joy even amongst chaos and depression. We make it possible to be happy even during the worst times of our lives.

One of the best ways we can start showing our gratitude and lifting our spirits is to start the practice of writing down the things for which we are grateful.

Gratitude Journal

A really easy way to make gratitude a daily practice in your life is to start a gratitude journal. I first started doing this in high school. It became a daily habit and I did it for many years. Unfortunately, I got out of the habit once I started having children and it took me many years to find it again. I like to take a few minutes before I go to bed every night to write at least five things I am grateful for in my journal.

I can honestly say that the happiest times in my life have been when I've looked for and written down the things that I appreciate from day to day. Daily gratitude really does turn our lives and our attitudes around within seconds.

The simple act of writing them down helps rewire our brains for more gratitude. It helps us remember the things that we appreciate about life. It allows us to appreciate what we've recorded that we might otherwise have forgotten, and preserves these memories for loved ones.

Having this daily habit also trains our minds to start looking for the good in every day. When we know that we have to write something positive in our journal at the end of the day, we will spend our day looking for those positive things to write down.

I have kept a few different kinds of gratitude journals. Sometimes I make lists and write down one-liners that express gratitude for something simple. In other books, I write down paragraphs and express details of events and things that I'm grateful for. You can write one thing a day, five things, ten things, etc. It doesn't really matter how many you write. What really matters is the way it makes you feel. When you feel grateful you are happy and that is the point of the entire exercise.

One really great way to revolutionize your *entire life* is to write one thing you are grateful for about each *specific category* in your life you want to improve. For example, I write one thing I'm grateful for about my body, my house, my relationships, my career, and one for general things. This way I am showing gratitude for every aspect of my life and attracting even better things to be grateful for each day.

These musings are really nice to have around when you have a bad day or are going through a hard time. You can read them, and they will take you back to those moments you were glad to experience. They will alleviate your current pain by reminding you of times when you didn't feel that pain. This will instantly help you feel like you are overreacting and that the "sun will come out tomorrow." It also helps to remind you nothing is permanent. No matter how hard your current situation might seem, it will eventually change.

There might come a day when all you can write in your gratitude journal is you are "grateful you can write." There are going to be good days on which it will be hard to fit the things you are grateful for on a page (or ten pages, if you're like me), and there will be days when a one-liner is all you can do. Become consistent and keep at it. Even when you can only find one line to write, just do it. The more you do it, the easier it will become to find the things in each day that are noteworthy and bring us joy. I promise you the more you write about being grateful, the more happiness you will feel in your life.

Little Black Book

Another aspect of your life that is totally worth your time is your relationships. Each relationship we have is a gift, whether it is a good gift or one that we are to learn from is up to us. Gratitude has been scientifically proven to improve our relationships and make us more attractive to good friends and to a better love life[9].

Apparently, there are people who keep a little black book about all the people they have dated and/or liked in their lives. It usually contains their name, address, and possibly information about why they liked them, or how/why the relationship ended or didn't work. Some keep a book about all the people they hate and what they don't like about them. That is a good recipe for insecurity and for not having any real friends. I'd like to recommend a different kind of black book.

While friendships are important to me, my relationships with my family members are the top priority of my life. Most of the time I struggle with the relationship with some of my kids, and occasionally, my husband has proven to be quite a handful.

A few years ago I was reading a book called *The Compound Effect* by Darren Hardy[10]. Although it is a book about finances, my biggest take-away from it saved my marriage. Mr. Hardy talked about several things that he did to show his love for his wife. At that time, my husband and I were going through a hard time in our marriage; I was struggling to remember why I married him. In the book, Darren said he wrote something he loved about his wife every day for a year into a little book for her. I thought that was a brilliant idea and decided to write down something I loved about my husband every single day for a year. I bought a tiny "black" book and diligently found a few minutes every day to record something he did to make me happy or that I noticed and was grateful for. I found this practice really enhanced my marriage and made me look for the good that was already there and find a deeper appreciation for all my husband did.

He had no idea I was writing this little book and I did a wonderful job of keeping it a secret for a little over a year. I was very proud of that. I started writing it in November, the month that always reminds us to be grateful, and then gave it to him for Christmas the following year. This little book was a treasure to me, and I hoped that by giving it to him it would spark in him a desire to do the same for me. He didn't, or hasn't, but I'm okay with that. I know that by looking for the good in him every day for a year, *I started a daily lifetime habit*. I discovered that while I was giving him this most thoughtful of gifts, I was really giving myself the gift of renewed love for my marriage. I found reasons to love him instead of reasons to be angry or find fault. I soon found myself feeling profoundly grateful for the man I married rather than remorseful.

I think every person needs to get into this habit and have something like a little black book to turn to and help them feel love and appreciation for loved ones.

I don't believe it's necessary to write it in a book, but if we at least look for the good in our partner (child, coworker, family, friend) we are bound to find it. When we express this, it will do something amazing for that relationship and will bring us a deeper connection and greater joy. This can be as easy as sending a nice text or putting a short love note in a lunch box. These are things each human being needs: connection, joy, and love. When we feel more love for ourselves, we will find it a lot easier to love other people as well.

The most important relationship we can cultivate while here on Earth is our relationship with ourselves. If you struggle with self-esteem or body image issues, like I did for most of my adult life, it would be great to start a little black book for yourself. You could write a few things every day that you like about yourself or that you are proud of. By looking for the good in yourself you will start feeling more confident and loving.

We are commanded to "love our neighbor as our self" but how many of us love ourselves? I know that by doing this simple thing for myself I have in turn learned to see my neighbor with much kinder and gentler eyes than before. Being grateful for our bodies will also help them to perform better for us and feel better.

Our relationships with people, including our self, the memories we make, and the feelings we have together are some of life's greatest treasures. You can feel more joy by spending quality time with the ones you love than by doing or owning any other thing. Every relationship has its ups and downs, its peaks and valleys. However, the more grateful you are for those relationships, the more ups than downs you will find.

When we train our minds to look for and appreciate the good in other people, they will start to do this for us as well. It is a win-win situation. You can never go wrong with expressing gratitude and finding the good in other people or things. I really wanted my children to learn the art of being grateful, and so I made up a fun game to regularly practice it with them.

The Grateful Game

When I am feeling down or there is a lot of tension at home (which is not rare), I have come up with a fool-proof way of lightening the mood and raising the positivity around us. This game is a simple yet profound one, much like Pollyanna, in the old Walt Disney movie *Pollyanna*[11]. It is a fun way to get everyone looking on the bright side again rather than fighting or finding fault. Pollyanna called it the "Glad Game," I call it the Grateful Game.

You start by having one person say what they are grateful for at that moment and then they have to say why. You basically fill in the blanks for the following: "I am grateful for _____ because _____."

You should aim at being as detailed as possible in your reasons why you are thankful for that particular thing; for the more praise you give to it, the greater you will feel.

For example, I could say: "I am grateful for the sunshine because it makes me feel warm. It gives the necessary light for the trees and plants to grow and produce food and oxygen. It makes me feel happy inside when the sun is out and helps me to see better. I love the warmth of sunlight when I close my eyes and look at it, and the feeling of power I get from knowing that the sun will always rise and set even when I can't see it. I love that it makes my skin look tanner and that it makes it bearable for me to get into a cold swimming pool." Etc. Etc. You don't have to be that specific or say that much, but I was giving a generous example for those overachievers who really want to have more fun in their lives.

You could also keep it simple and say something as easy as: "I am grateful for pizza because I love the way it tastes."

Kids really like this game and it is hilarious to hear what they have to say. It takes them out of a bad mood and makes them look at what they already have when they are feeling especially needy. I promise that if you are having a bad day, playing this game even for a minute will pick up the mood and lighten the atmosphere. Try to find things that are silly and taken for granted, kids love that. It teaches them to see how many things they really do have and to not expect so much. One of my daughters made us all laugh this past week when it was her turn to share something. She said, "I'm grateful for nostrils because they are fun to look at." Give it a try.

Another variation of this is to pretend all your wildest dreams have come true. You express joy and gratitude for the things you feel from having those dreams come true. For example: "I am so excited that we are going to Scotland next week; it is a dream come true!" even though you really aren't going on vacation, it is fun to dream and act as if. This exercise will help you gain momentum on making your dreams come true. We can all use help motivating ourselves once in a while.

In short, the best, easiest, and quickest way to instantly impact your life is to start being more grateful and expressing more gratitude. It has positive results in every aspect of your life. Remember how one of the benefits of being grateful was to ease muscle tension and toxic chemicals in our body? That leads us right into the next habit that saved my sanity: learning how to relax.

Parenting win:

After giving my kid a cup of juice (3-year-old) she said, "Thank you, Your Highness!"

-Amber Clark

Chapter Highlights:

- Being grateful is so simple you can do it any time anywhere, yet it is the most powerful thing you can get into the habit of doing.
- No matter what time of day, no matter where you are, gratitude can soothe your soul and make you feel great in an instant. At a minimum, we should start and end our day with gratitude.
- To really live a life with gratitude, we must really *feel* grateful. We must not only express thanks but do so in sincerity and with feeling.
- Gratitude changes your attitude, and attitude determines your altitude.
- A positive attitude can affect our health.
- In finding something to be grateful for, even in the hardest times, we can find hope and see that our lives get better.
- When we choose grateful thoughts rather than unkind or mean thoughts, we open the gates of our minds to take us away from our current realities and experience joy even amongst chaos and depression. We make it possible to be happy even during the worst times of our lives.
- A really easy way to make gratitude a daily practice in your life is to start a gratitude journal.
- Having a little black book in which to write about the good you find in others will improve any relationship.
- The most important relationship we can cultivate while here on Earth is our relationship with ourselves.

Actions to Take

- Write down a list of five things you are grateful for right now.

  1. _____

  2. _____

  3. _____

  4. _____

  5. _____

- Answer the following questions:

  1. What can I do today to start being more grateful?

     _____

     _____

  2. Which one action/habit from this chapter will I implement into my life starting now?

     _____

     Why? _____

     _____

     How? _____

     _____

- Place your hand on your heart and repeat the following phrase out loud, "*I am grateful to be a mom. No matter what my kids do or say, I am so blessed they are in my life.*"

HABIT TWO:
LEARN TO RELAX

"Sometimes the most productive thing
you can do is relax."
—Mark Black

"You don't always need a plan. Sometimes you
just need to breathe, trust, let go and
see what happens."
—Mandy Hale

Being a Mom is Super Stressful

Most of my years as a young mother are a blur to me even though it was only a few years ago. I lived in a constant state of panic, worry, and stress. You could say I was a frazzled, stressed out, hot mess. It was all I could do to stay awake during the day, let alone keep my kids alive and maintain my sanity.

There was a time when things got so bad I became what I considered to be a terrible mother. We had moved to a new state so my husband could start his first job fresh out of medical residency. It was a demanding time on both of us and it nearly tore us apart. I had no money, no energy, no friends or family within a seven-hour drive, and felt completely and utterly alone and desperate.

I was staying home with my five children, two of whom were in school by this time. The other three were less than a year, three years and four years old (these two were "Irish twins," exactly 12-months and five days apart.) Together they formed a team to try and destroy me. At least that is how I felt.

I hate to admit it, but it got to the point where I was so desperate for some sleep and quiet that I put a lock on their door and locked them in their room for nap time each day. I felt like I had to. After months of trying to get them to stay in the house during nap time, they kept trying to escape and go outside. This was not safe at all. We lived on a scary ridge that was extremely close to the road and the drivers never went the speed limit. Hardly a day passed that I didn't worry about my children's safety in that house. To keep them safe while the baby and I got a few moments of sleep, they were locked in their room. They tried all sorts of antics to get out, mostly gross things with the potty. I would put pull-ups on them and even left a potty-seat in their room. For a few weeks they refused to use either, and instead opted to paint the walls with their feces and to pee and poop in the air conditioning vent.

Yep, you read that right. It was the highlight of my young mothering years having to put on dish gloves to fish out their bowel movements from the vent. I was so desperate and devastated that I had children who could do such a thing.

I was in a constant state of feeling overwhelmed, alone, and like a hopeless failure of a mother.

No one likes to feel like that. If I had only known then what I know now, I could've saved myself from years of sadness and self-loathing. I could have had peace amongst the chaos and made lemonade out of the lemons I'd been dealt. What I perceived as bitter could have been sweet.

Perhaps you are like the younger version of me and feel stressed out by your little ones and your "job." If so, you are completely normal.

So many people are living life in a constant state of stress and frenzy. We run around from thing to thing and place to place, keeping so busy that we don't even allow ourselves time to breathe. This feeling makes it hard for us to find joy in the journey. Feeling stressed or anxious is usually not peaceful. It is painful.

Side Effects of Stress

It is no secret that most stress is not good for us. In fact, it is what is behind so many of our physical aches and pains. According to WebMD, the following are a few of the negative side effects of stress on our bodies:

- Low energy

- Headaches
- Upset stomach, including diarrhea, constipation, and nausea
- Aches, pains, and tense muscles
- Chest pain and rapid heartbeat
- Insomnia
- Frequent colds and infections
- Loss of sexual desire and/or ability[12]

In addition, Dr. Bruce Lipton, a famous cell biologist turned public speaker and author says, "Stress is the cause of at least 95 percent of illness and disease." (*Biology of Belief)*[13]

I don't know about you, but after a while of living with constant stress and pain, I got to the point where I knew I needed to change. I hated feeling stressed and what it was doing to my body and to my family.

I was determined to figure out *the source* of my stress and find healing. I didn't want to mask my pain or take a medication to numb how I felt. I wanted real answers. I desired to fix *the true reason* behind my problem *rather than addressing a symptom*. While I appreciate modern medicine and the relief it provides to many of us, I knew that *my problem* had to do with my thoughts and reactions rather than some kind of chemical imbalance or physical issue. I have learned that at the heart of almost every pain and distress I experience there is an underlying emotion or psychological limiting belief or pain. By learning how to self-evaluate and find the root cause of our issues we can often heal ourselves and save money to boot.

In order to evaluate my stress, I started asking myself some hard questions. Rather than reacting to everything that "stressed me out" I started wondering why

I was feeling such heavy emotion in such situations. Here is an example:

When my child would have a tantrum over not being able to find a sock in the morning before the bus came I used to go insane. They'd cry and cry for 20 minutes without getting up to look for one. I would yell and yell for them to get up and look, while frantically scouring the house for the missing sock. Both of us would be complete basket cases- they were screaming and crying like they were dying and I was screaming and crying, wanting to pull out every hair on my head.

This is where the self-evaluating questions come in. Why on earth was I completely losing my mind over a sock? Was I mad because I thought that my kid would miss the bus? Yes, but why? It would inconvenience me for an extra half hour of my day. Was that really worth pulling my hair out? OR was it something else?

Did I get so mad about the sock because it showed that I was a failure of a mother, not knowing where my kids' belongings were at every moment? I hated feeling like I wasn't in control. Was I a terrible mother because I couldn't properly take care of my kids? They were so unhappy! I thought it was my job to make them happy and therefore, the missing sock was making them unhappy and it was my fault.

I began diving further into these reflective thoughts. Why did I feel like it was my job to make my kids happy? Was it? Was their happiness more important than my own to the point that I should give up every joy and all my time to try and meet their needs? No, it wasn't. I was as important and valuable as them. Of course I wanted them to be happy, but not at my own expense. I soon realized that a missing sock doesn't mean that I am failing as a mother. An out-of-control, over-reacting kid didn't mean that I was a *bad* mom either. In fact, the only thing that was making me a *bad* mom *in that situation* was my over-reaction to it, or my lack of control. Did you notice that I put, "in that situation" in italics? That is because I want you to recognize that while we might have bad moments or overreactions, they do not define who we are. They are not permanent labels, they are temporary mistakes that we can improve upon.

I realized that I didn't have to lose my cool over a sock just because my kid did. I was supposed to be modeling to them how to respond under stress. I should not have been surprised at all that they were yelling and crying and losing control. I was doing the same thing. *Who were they learning from and whose example were they following?* **Mine!** I needed to learn how to stop letting all the small day-to-day things get under my skin and I needed to do it quickly. I knew that things couldn't get any better until I did.

It was an important part of my personal growth and I began by reading about stress. I learned several interesting things such as not all stress is negative.

My almost 3-year-old is in the phase of wanting to buckle herself in her car seat. She can't always get it done, so this time I just stepped up onto the running board in case she needed help. I didn't even touch her. She stopped what she was doing, looked me straight in the eye, pointed her finger at me and said, "Don't even!" Then went back to trying to buckle up. I was a little dumbfounded." Facebook Friend

---

Using Stress to Our Advantage

In her book, *The Upside of Stress*[14], Kelly McGonigal tells that stress doesn't have to be a bad thing in our lives. In fact, sometimes it can be a positive. If we learn to harness its power, it can help us meet deadlines and overcome problems in our lives. She says there are many positives to stress, but first we have to start looking at stress in a different way.

We need to figure out what is causing our stress and why. *Stress is really a way that we perceive a situation.* It is a lens we look through to see the world. It is like the windshield of our car getting hit by a rock. It can cause a little dent at first, but if it continues to get hit with more and more rocks or faces changes in temperature (emotions and hormones) often that little dent can cause a huge crack across the entire windshield, causing our view to become less clear and making it harder to find clarity on our journey.

We can change that lens when we are aware that we are looking through it. It is just as easy to change the windshield in our car as it is to change our perspective. It may take time and a little money, but it is so worth it in the end. If we don't fix the windshield, we could end up with shattered glass all over us.

This is where mindfulness comes to our rescue.

Being Mindful

Have you ever driven somewhere and when you arrived you realized you had no idea how you got there or what you were thinking about during the entire drive? That is distracted driving, getting lost in our thoughts, and not being aware. That is what it is like to live on cruise control and not really be present in our own lives.

Instead, we want to become obsessively aware of our thoughts and feelings and surroundings. We need to be more mindful.

Funny enough, the first book I ever read on mindfulness was written by the award-winning actress Goldie Hawn, a woman I knew from one of my favorite childhood movies, *Overboard*.[15] It was a little hard for me to take her book seriously when I would think of the movie, but once I got past that, I realized that she was really onto something. Her book is called *10 Mindful Minutes.*

Mindfulness is being more aware in our lives and trying to tune into our thoughts and become more cognizant of what we are experiencing throughout the day. After reading a few stories about mothers actually forgetting their babies in their cars, to the point of them passing away, it became apparent that too many of us are in desperate need of this lesson.

My mindfulness journey began by noticing the wind on my face, the sun beating down on me, the smells that penetrated my nose, etc. I soon realized that noticing the little things was quite lovely. I became more and more desirous to *notice every sensation in my life* and soon got really into it.

I made mindfulness a part of my morning routine by trying to be aware of individual parts of my body for five minutes. I would concentrate on my feet, my legs, my thighs, my chest, heart, shoulders, head, etc. As I thought about each place on my body I would give them thanks for functioning properly and allowing me to do what I needed to do. It felt great to become more aware of my body and my thoughts. I noticed I was growing more grateful for the things I experienced on a daily basis and was therefore feeling happier. I began to crave this feeling and wanted to learn more about it.

Being more mindful requires some effort, but is well worth it. Start by noticing the little sensations in your life and try to do it more and more frequently every day. Pay attention and become aware of your surroundings and your feelings.

I took a *Krav Maga* training class and the first thing they teach you in self-defense is to be very aware of your surroundings. When you leave a store or building, scan the area and know what is around you. Be alert and prepare your mind for possible scenarios.

This is how we should train our minds to become all the time, not just when preparing for danger. When we become more alive, alert, and aware, we are given many more opportunities to smell the roses in our lives and find the good. At first you will not have much control over your mind and awareness. However, with practice and time, you will get better at it.

It is similar to training a muscle. It gets stronger and easier the more you do it, so try to take a few minutes every day to be more aware of your thoughts and feelings. Take a moment when you are driving or waiting for something, or even when you are going to the bathroom, to turn off the noise and distractions in your life and quiet your mind. Become more aware of the recorded track of thoughts that is constantly going on in your mind. Notice what you are thinking about and try to learn how to harness, control, or change the things that are not allowing you to feel love for yourself or others.

Simply being aware of the moment can help you calm down and gain control. Being present in life helps you stress less and have more joy. When you are playing with your kids or having lunch with a friend make sure you put your phone away. When someone is talking to you, try to tune into what they are saying and not get distracted by what you want to say. This will strengthen your relationships and help you see the big picture in front of you rather than focusing on the cracks.

Slow Down and Take a Breather

Have you ever had a time when you were so stressed or anxious that you could barely breathe? I have, and it is not a good feeling, nor a good sign. Breathing is one of the best things we can do when we feel stressed or an anxiety attack coming. When you feel like you can't breathe, nothing is more important than being able to do so. Your body is trying to tell you to slam on your brakes and take a breath. A *deep breath*!

One of the best ways I have found to help me when I perceive stress is to deep breathe.

We are all breathing all the time, but you'd be surprised at how few of us really know how to breathe in such a way that aids us in obtaining optimal health. *Too many of us are shallow breathers and shallow breathing doesn't give us all the oxygen our brain needs to be super healthy.* It can keep our brain in a state of stress rather than peace. When we breathe in deeply for as little as five minutes a day, we can train our brain to respond differently and better.

Breathing deeply releases endorphins that calm our minds down and soothe our nerves. It also provides pain relief, by stimulating the lymphatic system which cleanses toxins in our bodies and improves our immunity and energy levels. These are all things that will improve our quality of life and even extend our lives.[16]

Any time I feel anxiety or stress coming on, I now deep breathe as soon as I feel it. This has alleviated my burdens immensely. My kids know if I start deep breathing around them, they are not acting how I want them too. They also know that if they are acting out of control or can't control their emotions, I will sit with them and aid them in slowly returning all of their attention to their breath. In doing so, we have curbed many tantrums and turned around a lot of stressful situations.

How to Deep Breathe

To properly deep breathe, you inhale through your nose until your belly gets as high and as full as it possibly can, then slowly exhale through your mouth as if the air were coming out of a straw. I like to imagine that my lungs are like a big balloon and I have to fill it up with each inhale. You don't want your chest to rise, but rather your lower abdomen to inflate. I prefer to lay down for this exercise, when I can.

I like to add some words to concentrate on during my deep breathing practice. When inhaling I think "faith," "serenity," or "relax," and when exhaling I blow out all "fear," "stress," or "tension." That way I am filling my mind with good things and releasing my body of anything negative. I have found this to be a very calming and soothing practice.

Whenever you feel the slightest pang of stress coming into your mind, take a few minutes to breathe in and out, and you will find greater clarity and satisfaction. You will release the chemicals in your brain that help with situations of freeze/flight/fright and you will react much better. Trust me. Try and fit this practice into your schedule every day.

Practice preventative breathing. I actually have a Breathe App on my watch that beeps once every hour to remind me to stop and slow down for a minute to take a deep breath. I find it good to be reminded as often as possible. The more you practice this, the calmer and less stressed you will feel.

It doesn't take very much time at all. You have to breathe all the time anyway, so you might as well do it the right way at least some of the time. Do it in the shower, on your drive home from work, when you are going to sleep, waiting in line, wherever, just do it. If you combine the act of deep breathing with that of mindfulness, you will quickly find yourself feeling more energy and enjoying greater peace. You will have learned a simple yet profound technique for finding calm in the eye of the storm.

Benefits of Deep Breathing

Deep breathing not only helps instantly reduce stress, but it has many other health benefits as well. According to recent science, breathing consciously increases your energy level, improves your respiratory system, and calms the nervous system. The nervous system determines how you feel throughout the day so that benefit alone will instantly help you feel good about yourself and your life. It also improves the lymphatic system (helps prevent colds and viruses), the cardiovascular system (decreases the risks of heart attacks), and the digestive system (allowing our bowels to perform their best).

As moms we all want to stick around and be as healthy as possible for our kids, if not for ourselves. We also want our kids to be healthy. The simple act of deep breathing every day is an easy way to instantly improve our health in many ways, allowing us to be better, more patient mothers. Teaching our children the practice will prevent illnesses and long-lasting effects of stress in their lives. They will learn from a young age how to handle hard situations. I sure wish I would've been able to teach my older kids this while they were little.

Deep breathing also:

- **Releases muscle tension.** I don't know about you, but my muscles often get tight and tense when I am around my kids or under a lot of stress.
- **Reduces our risk for depression.** I know many moms who are depressed and almost nothing seems harder to a depressed mother than taking care of children. Wouldn't it be great if you could prevent/alleviate/cure your depression by taking more regular deep breaths?
- **Slows down the aging process.** Breathing alone can make us feel and look younger. I know a lot of women who spend tons of money on beauty products to try and reduce wrinkles and make them appear youthful. If they'd breathe more deeply more often, they could save some serious cash and look better, too.
- **Assists in weight control.** Say what? Yep, you read that right. The act of breathing deeply provides extra oxygen to help burn excess fat and feed starving tissues and glands. [17] Sign me up!!

As you can see, deep breathing is another free and simple technique that will give you instant rewards for practicing it. Add this technique to other things that tend to help you relax, like bubble baths, movie night, a girl's night out, reading a good book, etc., and you will be feeling refreshed in no time.

Let's review what we have learned in this chapter. By being more mindful of our feelings and surroundings, and taking a few minutes to deep breathe every day, we can instantly improve our lives. Adding these to the daily practice of gratitude, we are still at less than ten minutes of your time. I think the benefits of doing so are pretty profound for such small and simple things.

Now that you know a few techniques about relaxing you are ready to move on to the next step of our journey: enjoying nature.

Chapter Highlights:

- So many people are living life in a constant state of stress and frenzy. We run around from thing to thing and place to place, keeping so busy that we don't even allow ourselves time to breathe.
- "Stress is the cause of at least 95 percent of illness and disease." *Biology of Belief*
- In order to evaluate my stress, I started asking myself some hard questions. Self-evaluation can be liberating.
- In her book, *The Upside of Stress*, Kelly McGonigal tells us that stress doesn't have to be a bad thing in our lives. In fact, sometimes it can be a positive.
- It is just as easy to change the windshield in our car as it is the change our perspective. It may take time and a little money, but it is so worth it in the end.
- Mindfulness is being more aware in our lives and trying to tune into our thoughts and become more cognizant of what we are experiencing throughout the day.

- Being mindful is similar to training a muscle. It gets stronger and easier the more you do it, so try to take a few minutes every day to be more aware of your thoughts and feelings.
- One of the best ways I have found to help me when I perceive stress is to deep breathe.
- Breathing deeply releases endorphins that calm our minds down and soothe our nerves. It also provides pain relief, stimulates the lymphatic system which cleanses toxins in our bodies and improves our immunity and energy levels.
- When you inhale, think "faith/serenity/peace" and when you exhale, release "fear/tension/stress."
- The simple act of deep breathing every day is an easy way to instantly improve our health in many ways.

Actions to Take:

1. Write down some things that currently stress you out:

   _____

   _____

   _____

   _____

2. Reflect on why these thing stress you out and what you can do about it:

   _____

   _____

   _____

   _____

3. Practice deep breathing right now. Take a minute to put this book down and focus only on your breath. Think of what your key words will be when you inhale and exhale (ie: faith/fear).

4. When can you implement the practice of deep breathing into your day?

   _____

   _____

5. Add the Breathe App to your phone or watch, if you can.

6. Place your hand on your heart and repeat out loud, "I am getting my stress under control. I am a positive role model for my children."

HABIT THREE:
ENJOY THE NATURAL THINGS IN LIFE

"In every walk of nature one receives far more
than he seeks."
—John Muir

"Look deep into nature, and then you will
understand everything better."
—*Albert Einstein*

My seven-year-old daughter recently ran into the bathroom and relieved herself. She had a huge smile on her face (the door was open and I could see her), when she yelled out, "Mom, are you writing about going pee in your book? I responded, "I don't know, why?" She said, "Because, it is so refreshing!"

I got a good laugh out of that. While it is true, there are other things that really provide me with the refreshing feelings moms desire. For me, the world around me does that.

Take a Ten-Minute Nature Walk:

There is something about being outside in nature that is very healing to our souls. When we take the time to go outside and put our phones and worries away for a while, we can instantly connect with the beauties the world has to offer. In turn, we will find ourselves feeling more grateful and happy. As we learn to enjoy nature, we learn to love our planet and as a result, we treat it better. We start to see we are connected to all living things and showing them love makes us feel more loveable. Since we are one with nature, we have a responsibility to take care of it and appreciate what it does for our souls.

In the book *Change Your Mind Change Your Life*, we read, "When we begin to see it is our responsibility to love all that is life, all that is living, we then begin to make a difference in expressing our love to all the animals, trees, and all of nature that makes up our environment."[18] I have learned that the more I go outside, the more I notice the songs of the birds, the whispers of the wind, and the absolute grandeur of it all. It is a great way to practice being mindful. These observations make me feel joyful.

We can and should go on walks regularly, not just for exercise, but for the benefit to our spirit. It is akin to the difference between leaving a car in the garage all year long versus getting it outside and driving in the fresh air. We need to leave our houses and comfort zones, to get regular fresh air, or we will get "rusty" and feel depressed.

When we look at nature in all of its forms and majesty we can recognize we are not alone in this universe and that there is something higher and more to life than our busy, race-to-the-next thing society. Observing the little things in the world around us can help us to slow down and appreciate life. We can feel joy when looking at a sunset, smelling the roses, watching the birds fly, listening to the cricket's chirp, seeing a squirrel jump from tree to tree, breathing fresh air, and being rejuvenated by the sun. To me, there is almost nothing more refreshing than drinking a cold glass of water while standing in the sunshine. Being outside helps us see God's hands in all things and seeing that helps you connect with Him. When you connect with Him, you feel more love for yourself, which brings you more joy!

Observe Animals

I have never been a dog person, but last Easter I caved to my kids' relentless begging for a dog and we bought a cute, little, yellow lab. We named him Benson. While there are many things I dislike about owning a dog such as the added responsibility on my plate (my kids have not exactly been the most loyal of feeders, cleaners, or walkers), I do love the fact that he makes me get outside and go for a walk. In fact, I love him for it.

If you have ever observed an animal or taken a dog on a walk, you can see they really live for each moment, they are perfect examples of mindfulness. They are not caught up in the past, nor worrying about the future. They are always seeing what is going on right here, right now.

Benson walks nearly every day. I am usually trying to get my own exercise, so I'm guiding him where I want to go, as fast as I want to go. Every once in a while, I let him call the shots and I go where he wants. It is a little disturbing that we don't make it very far- he is sniffing and licking and enjoying every single morsel of grass, rock, feces, dirt, snow, etc. that we encounter. He is happy just observing and experiencing every sensation our walks could possibly offer. He happily "smells the roses", even though I'd never bring him near our roses because I know he'd eat them! He enjoys everything that nature and the world has to offer him, and connects with as many things as he can. We can learn a lot from watching such animals follow their natural instincts.

Every time I am out there with Benson I like to observe how he behaves and what life must be like for a dog. It doesn't take a genius to notice he can see, hear, taste, and feel things that I cannot. Dogs have very keen senses and can teach us a lot about how to love.

I once heard a joke that goes something like this: "If you were to put your wife and your dog in the trunk of your car, who would be most happy to see you when you opened it?" I think it is safe to say the dog would be oblivious to how poorly you had behaved and would treat you the same as if you'd brought it to a dog park. The wife, not so much. Pets are an amazing example of unconditional love, getting over the bad things that happen quickly, and finding joy.

They are also the perfect example of how to slow down in life and enjoy what we have been given. Benson is never in a bad mood and always excited to see us. He is always full of energy and grateful for the time we give him, even when it is minimal at best. If we could all be a little more like Benson and less frenzied and fast-paced, we'd all be a lot happier. We might even have more energy and life, also like Benson. When I have spent some quality time outside, I always feel better emotionally and physically.

It doesn't take a lot of time outside to rejuvenate your soul and help you feel connected and more alive. Some of my most sacred experiences have happened as a result of reflecting upon nature. It is important for me that I leave my technology at home or at least tucked away during my walk. It is too much of a temptation to look at the phone and miss the sunset; to answer a call rather than to hear the rush of the wind; or to take a picture rather than enjoying and being present in the moment. Occasionally, however, it comes in handy.

Sacred Reflections

Last year I had a profound experience while enjoying my walk around our pond. Our pond was not full and was looking rather disgusting at the time. It had about four to five feet of water at the deepest part and was muddy and gross. However, it was still remarkably peaceful, and I loved watching the still water reflect the sunlight. I saw a piece of wood in the water and had a deep desire to see if I could hit it with a rock. I tried, and as I did I became mesmerized by the ripple effect. I sat in awe of the thousands of ripples and waves that one little rock made.

Then I heard a voice, as small and still and piercing as ever, and knew it was the Spirit of the Lord. He told me that each one of us is like that little rock and have a much bigger influence on the world than we could possibly understand.

I thought for a moment and knew I needed to record a video of the ripple effect and share what I had learned on Facebook. I had a thought I might say something like, "please disregard the ugly muddy water and watch for the moral of the story," when the voice continued, "No, Nichole; the mud is part of the story. Don't you see? The muddy water is the world. It is up to each individual to make as much of a ripple, or difference, as they can in the dirty, wicked world." I watched as the ripples reached the furthest edge of the pond and wondered at the beauty of that moment.

We are more influential than that rock, and it is up to us to make the world a better, cleaner place to be. We make a much bigger impact than we think, in our families, our communities, and our world. I learned that the hard way a few times over the past years.

Hard Lessons

The first time was when I found out a few days before Christmas that my fun-loving uncle had committed suicide and left his wife and six children fatherless. It was devastating and far reaching. People that we didn't even know were reaching out to the family and experiencing the loss with us. We still feel his loss deeply, though it has been a few years now.

One summer I saw the same thing happen as two popular young men in our community that graduated high school in 2016, also committed suicide. Our little town came out in droves and filled up the entire high school gymnasium with support and love for the family of one of the boys. I didn't personally know the boy, but I knew his sister and father, and I was deeply moved and saddened by the experience. He had no idea who I was and never will, but I will always remember him and the impact one life made on our community and on me.

The other young man happened to be a previous member of the high school marching band that my daughter had just joined. The tragedy occurred while she was attending her first band camp. In order to help the students in the band grieve, they brought in some grief counselors or preachers. My daughter tells how the band formed a circle of love and support in which the students were allowed to come forward and tell how they were feeling, in a safe environment. She was taken aback (as was I) that when they asked the kids, "Who here has had suicidal thoughts or desires to hurt themselves?" more than 75% of the students admitted to feeling that way. If this is happening in small town rural Ohio in the middle of the Bible Belt- I don't even want to know the national statistics. What a tragic and horrifying mindset besets so many of our youth. Our kids are in desperate need of learning self-love and acceptance!

I will never look at my kids, my life, and myself the same after witnessing the effects of suicide or death.

It is a tragedy that is all too common and needs to be talked about and prevented. I believe that the message I received at that pond is so pertinent and needed in our day. Without knowing their own worth, people lose hope and feel like they don't matter. Nothing could be further from the truth. That is what initially sparked in me the desire to write this book. Spending quality time out in nature helps us feel more of our innate unconditional worth in the world.

Facebook

I had another revelation as I pondered the ripple effect at the pond. I realized for the first time that Facebook had become a negative addiction. I'd wait all day for someone to "like" me. I was using the likes and comments of other people to fill my need for feeling loved. It always fell short and I often felt like a failure or like I wasn't popular enough. It wasn't until the day after the pond that I was sitting in the early hours of the morning checking Facebook, when I knew I had to delete it from my phone and replace it with a much better habit.

I felt the Spirit tell me, "Delete Facebook from your phone." I tried but couldn't do it the first time. In fact, I got on Facebook and changed the settings so that what I posted was for my eyes only and I couldn't get likes or comments because no one else was allowed to view them. However, the Spirit was not satisfied, and after the third prompting I finally obeyed and deleted it from my phone. That was over a year ago now and I have never regretted listening to that prompting.

Getting rid of the temptation to compare myself to the best posts of others and to feel less than them was one of the best decisions of my life. We all like to share the highlights of our lives on social media, making it appear like we are great mothers, or have it all together. We can post a picture of what looks like a positively clean kitchen, while the rest of the house around us is in shambles, and no one on social media would ever know. What we claim to be like on social media is often not natural, but fake to keep up appearances. It often leaves us feeling worse, rather than better.

I still have a Facebook account, but only installed on my laptop. It is no longer an addiction; I only use it sparingly, and not to fill a void I had for love. I no longer need that, as I have learned how to love myself fully and don't care as much about what people think of me.

Instead of using Facebook as a filler, I am now utilizing it as a tool to help other women. It is my mission to inspire, uplift, and help as many women as I possibly can. For that reason, I have started a Facebook group in which moms can find tips and tricks and feel like they belong and are loved.

Since deleting that kind of temptation from my phone, I have been growing in self-love and confidence every day. I have been able to change my perspective by looking through a new lens- one that tells me I am worthy and don't have to fit into the mold of the world. Sometimes we try so hard to fit into the world that we don't fit into our own skin. Meaning, we don't feel comfortable being who we were born to be and thereby deny ourselves the joy of recognizing our unique inner beauty. That is just one of the many benefits of being outside in nature and letting the tranquility and abundance of it soak into your bones.

Abundance & Benefits

Living in an ecosystem in which it rains frequently has made me see how rain is so majestic and powerful. In fact, all of nature seems to be overflowing with abundance. When we observe the "lilies of the field" or the weeds that grow without any human aid, we can easily see we are not in control of the elements. We learn there is a natural abundance in all things in which God is in control. We feel in our bones the sense of peace and calm that comes from relying on Him rather than fretting and worrying about our next meal or month.

Another random little tidbit I have learned about spending more time out in nature is it is great for our eyesight. My optometrist told me if I'd have my kids spend more time in the sun and less time inside, they might be able to prevent the need for glasses. I think that is pretty remarkable. Sunshine also fills us with light. It is like plugging ourselves into an outlet and recharging. It can give us energy and make us feel really good as long as we observe proper sun care. [19]

According to modern science, sunlight helps us release more serotonin, which is responsible for brightening our mood and alleviating depression. Sunlight also helps to regulate our blood pressure, boost our vitamin D intake, and feel more energy. Being outside at night can also help us increase the hormone of melatonin, which helps us sleep better.[20]

Reflecting on this beautiful Earth we are blessed to live on really helps us to receive personal revelation as to how to improve our lives and enjoy greater peace and less stress. It is beneficial to us both spiritually and physically.

After a nice walk or any physical activity, the absolute best thing we can and should do is drink some water.

Frequently Visit the Fountain of Life: Stay Hydrated

While it may appear inconsequential and too simple, staying hydrated is often overlooked. The lack of proper hydration can be extremely detrimental to our overall health and well-being.

In the book *Water Cures: Drugs Kill*, Fereydoon Batmangheldij says, "There is a medical breakthrough that is not reaching the public through our medical schools or health maintenance organizations: the discovery that chronic unintentional dehydration is the primary cause of pain and disease in the human body, including cancer. The reason these traditionally trusted institutions do not celebrate this scientific discovery and refuse to use it to help the sick and the uninsured poor in our society is obvious. There would be no money in it for them." [21]

"Chronic dehydration does not have the sudden and intense nature of the acute form, it affects nearly 75% of Americans and can result in many serious health problems."[22] That means that three out of every four people we meet are suffering needlessly.

"Our bodies are almost 70% water by weight. Almost every organ in our body is largely made up of water, and our blood is 83% water." In his book, *Water: The Ultimate Cure*[23], Steve Meyerowitz states that, "If your body's water content drops by as little as 2%, you will feel fatigued. If it drops by 10%, you will experience significant health problems. Losses greater than that can be fatal."

I was pretty alarmed by these statistics. I have always loved water and tried to drink enough of it every day, preferring it to any other drink. However, I know a lot of people who hardly drink any water at all during the day. I wish they knew that by drinking more water they could solve many of their health issues. It would save them so much money and pain.

"Why do we drink water? Because we can't eat it."

"Sometimes I drink a glass of water just to surprise my liver."

—Jokes found on Google

What Do You Drink the Most?

I have been attending a bible study class with other women and we always start with a get-to-know-you question. One week the question was, "What is your favorite drink?" I instantly thought of water, hands down it is my favorite beverage all of the time. However, as I listened to about 20 other women's answers I found that I was apparently the only one in the room with that opinion about water. Most preferred coffee and soda. I was shocked.

I found out a woman who I deeply respect and love to pieces, "can't stand the taste of water!" I was astounded by that statement. I can't understand how someone could not like water, but apparently it is fairly common.

Water is not only the best thing for our bodies and our health, but without it we would die. Even our brains are 75% water and our bodies need it to survive. Water literally gives life to every living thing on the planet and we need to be grateful for it and to drink it as much as we can. Every disorder from headaches, cramps, heartburn, depression, generalized fatigue, constipation, allergies, fibromyalgia, joint pain, hypertension, and even autoimmune diseases can be the result of dehydration.[24]

A simple way to tell if you are drinking enough water is to look at your urine. In fact, observing the things that come out of your body and into the toilet is one of the best indicators of health. If your urine is a light-yellow color, not clear and not bright, you know you've been consuming the right amount of water. You should be drinking at least half your body weight (in ounces) of water every day. That means if you weigh 200 pounds, you should be drinking 100 ounces of water (which is more than 10 cups a day).

If you are like my friend and don't like water, there are several things you can add to make it taste better. Essential oils, lemons or berries, cucumbers, or fizz packets all change the flavor drastically. In addition, there are now carbonated and flavored water options at any grocery store, so we are low on excuses for why we can't stay hydrated. Water is the only drink that truly and fully hydrates our bodies.

When we do not drink enough water, what are we drinking? Why?

Sugary Drinks and Our Health

With five children and a minimum of two visits to the dentist every year for each of them, not to mention time with orthodontists, I spend a lot of time looking after my children's teeth. It seems like every time we go, the dentist warns me to stop giving my kids sugary beverages. This always shocks me because I don't give them sugary beverages, and rarely even have them in our house. In fact, we pretty much drink only water and use milk for cereal and occasionally milk and cookies. Other than that, I only buy soda when we are having a party or other people over.

If my kids can keep getting cavities from *not* drinking sugary beverages, it makes me wonder what other families are dealing with. After doing some simple google searches to see how many sugary beverages are consumed each year and what it is doing to us, I was pretty alarmed. Sugary drinks have a much more harmful effect than you might guess.

First of all, what is a sugary drink? I think many mothers might be surprised what is on the list. According to an article by *The Nutrition Source* at Harvard's School of Public Health, "The term 'soft drink' refers to any beverage with added sugar or other sweetener, and includes soda, fruit punch, lemonade and other "-ades," sweetened powdered drinks, and sports and energy drinks."

I wondered how much of this sugary stuff Americans are drinking? The article continued, "On any given day, half the people in the U.S. consume sugary drinks; 1 in 4 consume at least 200 calories from such drinks; and 5% drink at least 567 calories—equivalent to four cans of soda.

According to Harvard's figures from the beverage industry, soft drink makers produce 10.4 billion gallons of sugary soda pop each year. That's enough to serve every American a 12-ounce can every day, 365 days a year."[25]

That is a lot of sugar! I had no idea that so many people drank so much of the stuff. I wonder if people know the real effects such drinking habits are having on their bodies? Do they know that sugary drinks not only hurt our teeth, but affect our weight as well?

I was recently diagnosed with gestational diabetes, and as a result have had to go without sugar and consume very few carbs. I was alarmed to see that many of the things that we eat on a regular basis were loaded with sugar. As mothers, we try to feed our kids healthy things, but often unintentionally give them the exact opposite. When I started looking at what was in some of the things that we normally eat and drink, it was pretty disturbing. I was really surprised at the amount of sugar that seems to be added to everything, from milk and apple juice, to syrup for pancakes and waffles. I was also pleasantly surprised by the fact that I didn't gain any weight the last four months of pregnancy (a far cry from my first five pregnancies), simply by watching what I eat. That was one blessing I found from having diabetes.

"Two out of three adults and one out of three children in the United States are overweight or obese, and the nation spends an estimated $190 billion a year treating obesity-related health conditions. Rising consumption of sugary drinks has been a major contributor to the obesity epidemic." [26]

A recent article on *livestrong.com* states that "By the end of one year, replacing just one sugary drink a day with water can cut 73,000 calories from your diet for a potential weight loss of 21 pounds -- without dieting." [27]

If you could lose twenty pounds or more in a year by simply replacing one sugary beverage with water a day, would you do it?

We live in such a blessed time in the history of the world where all we have to do is turn a faucet to have running water. It is a privilege we should never take for granted. We use water for everything, and it is a necessary ingredient in almost everything that we use to live. Our bodies cannot function properly if we aren't fully hydrated. A lot of people are regularly dehydrated and don't even know it. By being aware of how much water we consume each day, and getting at least five to eight glasses of it, we will feel refreshed and hydrated all day, which will give us more energy. Increased energy means more time to do what we enjoy! What mom doesn't want more of that?

Again, it takes very little time out in nature to experience significant improvements in our lives. By taking a mindful nature walk and drinking more water, we can soothe our spirits and replenish our self-worth and hydration in a matter of minutes.

Water is one of my favorite things to look at, to be in, and to drink. Some people fear water. When my kids were younger and couldn't swim I sure did. Sometimes there are things in nature that we fear but facing them can bring amazing blessings to our lives as well. That leads us to the fourth, life-changing habit.

Chapter Highlights:

- When we take the time to go outside and put our phones and worries away for a while, we can instantly connect with the beauties the world has to offer. In turn we will find ourselves feeling more grateful and happy.
- We can and should go on walks regularly, not just for exercise, but for the benefit to our spirit.
- We are not alone in this universe and there is something higher and more to life than our busy race-to-the-next-thing society.
- If you have ever observed an animal or taken a dog on a walk, you can see that they really live for each moment; they are perfect examples of mindfulness.
- It doesn't' take a lot of time outside to rejuvenate your soul and help you feel connected and more alive. Some of my most sacred experiences have happened as a result of reflecting upon nature.
- We make a much bigger impact than we think, in our families, our communities, and our world. The ripple effect is real.
- Facebook can become a negative addiction. Be aware of using the likes and comments of other people to fill your need for feeling loved.

- When we observe the "lilies of the field" or the weeds that seem to grow without any human aid, we can easily see that we are not in control of the elements. We learn that there is a natural abundance in all things in which God is in control.
- Sunlight helps us release more serotonin, which is responsible for brightening our mood and alleviating depression.
- The lack of proper hydration can be extremely detrimental to our overall health and well-being. "Chronic dehydration affects nearly 75% of Americans and can result in many serious health problems."[28]
- "By the end of one year, replacing just one sugary drink a day with water can cut 73,000 calories from your diet for a potential weight loss of 21 pounds -- without dieting." [29]

Actions to Take:

1. Go for a nature walk today and observe an animal or something around you. Write down what you observed and how it made you feel:

   _____

   _____

   _____

2. Make an action plan for how you will spend more time in nature on a regular (if not daily basis).

   _____

   _____

   _____

3. Pay attention to how many glasses of water you drink every day, and the color of your urine. If you are not getting at least 8 cups, how can you drink more?

   _____

   _____

   _____

4. If you are addicted to sugary beverages, try replacing one drink a week with water, then work your way down to one replacement per day.

5. Place your hand on your heart and repeat out loud, "I deserve to be healthy both physically and emotionally. I commit to taking care of my mind and body."

HABIT FOUR:
REPLACE CRITICISM & COMPARISONS WITH COMPLIMENTS

"You have been criticizing yourself for years and it hasn't worked. Try approving of yourself and see what happens."
—Louise Hay

"We all have the tendency to believe self-doubt and self-criticism, but listening to this voice never gets us closer to our goals. Instead, try on the point of view of a mentor or good friend who believes in you, wants the best for you, and will encourage you when you feel discouraged."
—Kelly McGonigal

Who is Your Very Worst Enemy?

Have you ever had to face your biggest fear? Most of us have at least one thing that we fear more than anything else. For some it is spiders, for others it is a job loss, death, a car accident, heights, being cheated on, etc. For me, it is snakes. I hate them with a passion. I get all tangled up inside just thinking about the slimy, slithering serpents and feel like they have a paralyzing effect on my entire body. I can't think when I am around them and certainly don't feel safe. I can't even stand seeing them on TV or in a picture. They strike a part of my heart that no other living creature seems to be able to. I don't really know how to get over it, and frankly, I don't even know if I want to try.

One day several years ago, I was preparing to move our things from our rental house to our first house that we'd been building for the past year. We had been renting for more than ten years and it was finally time to start planting some roots and make a home for our family of seven. I was really excited and very anxious to get out of this particular rental. We had had issues with mice and bugs, flooded carpets, and a plethora of other rather disgusting things (some that I mentioned earlier) that I don't care to mention or remember.

I was ready to start a new chapter in my life and move on and get over this old place. I began packing up our old, VHS movies that we collected with our five young children, taking them a few at a time from the built-in bookshelf by the fireplace and placing them carefully into the packing box. Yes, we had only VHS until a few years ago, as we were too poor to afford anything else.

As I reached to get the classic dinosaur movie, *Land Before Time*, from the bottom (which had no shelf), I was met with one of my worst fears. There, cuddled behind the video tapes, was a small, yet terrifying, snake, waiting to give me the scare of a lifetime. I jumped up, raced out of the room, grabbed my kids and my keys, and got as far away from the house as possible. I know now that I handled this situation in about the worst way possible, but hey, when we are faced with our deepest fears, we don't always think clearly.

When we got home, the snake was nowhere to be found. For weeks after that encounter, I felt uneasy and unsafe in our home. I knew that snake was somewhere inside, but didn't know where. I was counting down the days until we got to move, so anxious to get away from the bad memories and especially the scary snake. I couldn't sit on the couch without my heart beating a little faster. What if the snake came out from under it? I couldn't sit on the toilet without first looking inside and all around, terrified the sneaky serpent would be watching me with its beady eyes. I felt like I had to wear armor and boots to get out of bed in case it was lurking below. In short, I was a basket-case, knowing that my worst enemy was near and yet undetectable. I was driving myself crazy.

About three weeks after finding the little nightmare-inducing serpent, I went to pick my three-year-old daughter up from preschool, with my one-year-old in tow. We had a lot of groceries to bring in from the car and I had my arms more than full. I unlocked the door for my girls to go inside. I went back to the car to start hauling in our purchases. As I started walking back towards our rental house, the older daughter came running out of the house as fast as her chubby legs could carry her, screaming, "Snake! Snake!"

Upon hearing those words, I went numb. I stood there, paralyzed, unable to move. My heart was beating out of my chest. The fear that I had refused to face had returned to haunt me. Remembering that my one-year-old was still inside, I unleashed the protective Mama Bear inside me. I knew that I couldn't run from my enemy, nor let it stay in the house this time. I had to free myself from the daily fear of its presence once and for all. I put the groceries down, ran to the garage and got a baseball bat and a broom, and entered enemy territory. My heart was pounding, and I was scared to death, but I garnered enough warrior within to face the little demon.

It was sprawled out on the linoleum floor in my kitchen, acting like it belonged there. The snake kept flicking its tongue out at me, taunting me, as if it had all the power. Luckily it was only about ten feet away from the door, and on smooth floor that would make it easy to move. I slowly walked toward my worst enemy with plans to annihilate it and empower myself enough to never be afraid of another snake again. I brought the broom right up to it and started sliding it toward the door. I wanted to hit it with the bat outside so as not to have to clean up the mess. It tried to slither away from me and even tried looking at me, but I was all in. I knew that if I didn't face this fear today, I would have to keep living with it the rest of my life. As we got closer to the door, I swept it a little too hard and it flew out of the door and fell straight into the crack between two deck panels. I couldn't reach it to kill it, but at least I knew that it was out of the house.

That experience, though it didn't end the way I had hoped (yet I was secretly glad I didn't have to kill anything), has taught me a lot about life and about facing our enemies and our fears. It empowered me enough to know that I can survive a snake, and perhaps things that are a lot more life-threatening and terrifying. I have been able to look back on that experience and mentally bless that snake for giving me the chance to change for the better and stop beating myself up about being a scaredy-cat. That day I felt like I transformed from wimp to warrior.

The Real Enemy

Since then I have realized that there are far worse things in life that strike dread in my heart than a simple snake. We deal with terrorist attacks, massive public shootings, gangs, drugs, affairs, diseases, and so many things that are terrifying on a regular basis in today's world. While those big things are terrifying, odds are we will never personally encounter them. However, sometimes the little things, like the snake, fester so much inside our souls and our subconscious minds, often without us even knowing they are there that they do much more damage to us.

I have found that the snakes of life are all around us, even in our very homes. They are sneaking their way into our bedrooms, our television sets, our relationships, our literature, and most terrifying, they often control our minds. Often, we are completely unaware of their presence and we have no idea how close they really are.

We usually think of our own worst enemies as things or people that are far away and nowhere near us. We like to picture them as a different culture or race, living in a far-off land where they will have a very hard time getting to us. However, the more I live, the more I see that we are often surrounded by enemies. With school shootings and bullying becoming more and more frequent, with theft and violence being commonplace, it is hard to feel safe anywhere anymore. Many of us are dealing with a very strong enemy every single day without even knowing it. We look at this person all the time and even have to take care of them and meet their needs. This person knows our deepest, darkest secrets, they know how to push our buttons and make us feel horrible, and they can read our thoughts. If that is not scary enough, they know every text we send, every show we watch, and every dream we have hidden inside.

Most of us would never think of this person as our worst enemy. We might even see them as our friend, our ally, the one who has been with us through the best and the worst of times. Yet, similar to the case of the child being abused by the one that should love them most, this person, whom we should be able to trust more than anyone, is often the biggest enemy we will ever face. Have you guessed who it is yet? If not, let me give you a clue... all you have to do is look in the mirror and you'll see them.

Awaken the Cheerleader

Sadly, for many of us, the most terrifying enemy we will ever have is ourselves. We can be our own worst critic, beat ourselves up over the simplest of things, and make ourselves feel more unsafe than anything else. We can find fault in ourselves easier and faster than any other person, and often are so entrenched in the programming of criticism and fault-finding that we don't even know we are doing it. For this reason, *we* are very often *the biggest hurdle* most of us will have to get over in our lifetime.

We all have demons and inner critics lurking in the corners of our minds, controlling our behavior and beating us up. In order to face these sneaky demons we first need to learn how to recognize them for who and what they are. Then we can "get over" them and replace them with better, more empowering beliefs about ourselves.

The next life-changing habit is to stop criticizing all the things that we think are wrong with ourselves and to start complimenting and building on the things that we are doing well. We will dive into ways that we can replace the desire to bully and beat ourselves up with tools that will empower and awaken the cheerleader within us. Once the cheerleader within is awakened, we can start conquering our fears and learn how to be our own best friend.

Recognizing the Enemy Within

Like the little snake comfortably curled up behind one of my daughter's favorite movies, most of us have an inner demon silently getting way too comfortable inside of us. Unless we become aware of their presence, we might never even know they exist. We can go on and on with our daily routines, continuously and unsuspectingly feeding this inner enemy. We gladly give them food and shelter and allow them to grow in strength and control, while our inner cheerleader is hibernating.

We feed this demon every time we listen to their criticisms, each time we succumb to feeling like we are not "good enough," and when we believe their lies rather than fighting for the warrior within. The critic within resembles the evil in the world, or our ego. It teaches us a lot of lies and limiting beliefs. It truly believes that only a small few are destined for greatness, when in reality, we were all born to succeed and fill a need in the world. The first step in getting rid of the enemy within is to recognize they exist, who they are, and when they strike.

This is yet another habit where mindfulness comes in handy. Mastering the art of being in the moment and observing your thoughts and feelings can aid you in overcoming your worst critic.

One of my favorite movies from childhood was *Rigoletto*. It tells a powerful tale similar to that of *Beauty and the Beast,* in which a rich man is cursed on the outside for being ugly on the inside. He has to wait a very long time before he finds someone who will choose to defend him (which would break the spell), rather than leave him. A little girl is chosen for the job, and after he yells at her and shows his "beastly" side, she finds the beauty in him. He sings her a very touching and powerful song, called, *The Curse*[30]. If you have never heard the song, I highly encourage you to look it up and listen. It is amazing. The lyrics tell a wonderful story. The beast explains that *often the worst curse or spell we'll ever have to break free from is **the one we give ourselves***. When we see the power we have, can realize that *we are the **only ones** that can free ourselves from whatever curse we have been given*. We are our own worst villains- worse than any sorcerer or evil wizard.

Locked within ourselves, we each have the key to set ourselves free from the critical, depressing pattern of self-loathing and bullying.

Our inner critics come in many shapes and sizes, and they are unique for each of us. They target whatever it is that we secretly hate the most about ourselves, and feed on our fears.

I Hate My Body

For many, the struggle comes when looking at or thinking about their bodies.

For the majority of my adult life it seems that not an hour went by that I wasn't worried about, obsessed with, or insecure about my body. Bringing five children into the world didn't exactly do my body any favors and it took me about five years after having my last baby to get back to my goal weight. It is hard to fit exercise in when you have young children and feel tired all the time. However, it is possible, as you will find out later on in this book.

I am not in the minority when it comes to body loathing either. According to recent statistics, approximately 91% of women are unhappy with their bodies and resort to dieting. Only 5% of women naturally possess the body type often portrayed in the media. At least thirty million people of all ages and genders suffer from an eating disorder in the U.S. Every 62 minutes at least one person dies as a result of an eating disorder. This epidemic is trickling down to the children in our lives as well. Over half of teenage girls and a third of the boys are using restrictive measures to lose weight at any given time. Even 46% of 9-11 year-olds are sometimes, or very often, on diets. [31] [32] [33]

I don't know about you, but most of those statistics both shocked and saddened me.

So many people hate the way they look. I have heard people, including myself, complain about *every single body part*. People hate their ears, their eyes, their chin, their hair, their eyebrows, lips, etc.—and I've only touched on the head and face here! Women worry about their chest size, stomach area, and thighs. Mothers struggle to get back to their pre-pregnancy bodies and feel like failures or like their bodies are no longer beautiful after giving birth. Having children changes our bodies, whether we like it or not. However, we should be proud of what our bodies can do and be grateful for the lives they allow us to bring to the world. We can all think of at least one famous celebrity who didn't like the way they looked and literally went under the knife to have it changed. Many times, the changes made by plastic surgery actually make the person look worse and take away what we love most about them.

Unfortunately, the problems and things we criticize don't end with our bodies.

Do You Measure Up?

Did you know that a recent survey shows that around 80% of Americans are not satisfied with their lives and really don't like their day jobs? I couldn't find any statistics about moms, but my guess would be that young moms suffer a lot internally. With the abundance of comparisons going on through social media and everywhere we go, it is a wonder that we can even keep afloat sometimes. We compare our worth to what we think other people have just from a few photos or posts. We do the same thing in real life.

There is a tendency for each of us to mentally "size up" or critique everyone in a room upon entering it. This can happen within seconds as we find ourselves mentally checking every other person in our environment to see how we measure up. Within a few minutes we judge whether we are the big one, the small one, the fittest one, the ugly or pretty one, and so on. This practice is socially acceptable and normal. It is also sad. *We have too many critics in this world.*

Retraining the Needy Critic

Learning to retrain our inner critics to not only stop tearing our own life apart, but that of perfect strangers and good friends as well, isn't as hard as you might think. This habit of finding the good in ourselves and others does not take a long time. As I just explained, we make judgments of others within seconds of meeting them based solely on their looks. It is time to learn a new game.

Rather than sizing others up to see how we are either better or worse than them, we can start looking for only the good. When we find something that we love or like about someone else, we often feel jealous or unworthy. We might find ourselves trying to find fault with them or hearing our inner critic telling us how we will never be as good as them. Here is where we can make a simple change.

When we notice the voices of the inner critics (our own worst enemies) we can simply ask them to leave our minds by watching them float away from us like a cloud in the sky. Since we are only able to consciously think of one thing at a time, we can then replace those harsh critical thoughts with ones of praise. Doing so will lift our spirits and begin to rewire our brains for self-love and success rather than ripping ourselves (or others) apart and feeling bad.

For example, when we pass someone on the street and hear the critic within say, "She is fat," we can tell our mind to let that thought go and instead focus on something like, "I like her shoes." If you cannot find one good thing to think or say about her, simply turn your head and attention away from her and look at something that you can find the good in. The same approach applies to you—if that person you see on the street is yourself (your reflection in a mirror or window). Instead of indulging in criticism, you can train your inner critic to notice something you like about yourself. We will talk more about that a little later.

When I was a newlywed, I took a test from the book, *The Five Love Languages*[34] and learned that one of the ways that I feel loved is by hearing words of affirmation. I like compliments and thrive on hearing things that other people think are good about me (although I'm getting a lot better at not needing it). When I go too long without hearing anything good from anyone else, I find myself feeling down. There have been times when my "love tank" was running on empty. During those times, I would become needy and rather obnoxious. Desperate for any attention, I'd go out of my way to get a compliment. I would get dressed and put on more makeup than usual, make elaborate meals, then clean like a madwoman, all in attempts to hear something positive from my husband. Sometimes it would work, and I'd get something out of him, but more often than not, my silent expectations were not met. This often left me feeling worse.

After doing that for so long, I started to feel drained and unloved. I felt like I was overworked and underappreciated, and I had a chip on my shoulder. I started to question why I did anything. What was the point of folding laundry if no one noticed (until I messed up)? Why cook meals when no one said they tasted good? Why clean the toilets when they'd just be dirty again within the hour? Heck, why change the dirty diaper, if they were just going to poop again? It's not like the baby was thanking me.

I started to have a very negative approach to motherhood and homemaking. The lack of compliments or acknowledgment of all that I did had me down in a bad way. I needed help and I needed hope.

If you have felt that, or currently feel that, there is hope for you! You need not feel that way ever again.

If you have the same love language as me and have blamed your lack of feeling loved or appreciated on others (for not telling you what they love about you) you can stop. You can make the choice right now, to become your own cheerleader and build yourself up rather than continue on the misery track.

Learning that I was not a victim to a lack of love from others, but that I have complete control over how I feel and react in any given situation absolutely changed my life. I now try to take full responsibility for the way I feel at all times (it is a learning process). No one else has that power over me, and the same goes for you.

You do not need to wait for a compliment from anyone but yourself. You can make yourself feel loved and appreciated, and you can do it at any time and in any place. You cannot blame the way that you feel about yourself on anyone but yourself. You always get to choose how you feel and think. When you learn to take responsibility for your feelings, you gain a lot more control over those feelings quickly.

What is stopping you from turning your inner critic into your inner cheerleader? When you notice yourself going back to the old habits of ripping yourself or others apart, stop yourself in your tracks. Replace those negative thoughts and phrases with new empowering and uplifting ones.

Find out how you feel loved then do those things for yourself. If your love language is quality time, spend some quality time doing something you love! Treat yourself like your very own best friend. Give yourself a break. Buy yourself a gift. Take some time off to light a candle and eat some brownies and ice cream while watching your favorite movie. Treat yourself like the perfect date, and you will soon find that you don't need anyone else to do it for you.

External circumstances need no longer have any control over how you feel internally! It is such a liberating thing to come to understand. As a bonus, your children will see your example and follow your lead. After all, they love you and want you to be happy.

If we could just see ourselves through our children's eyes, how would we feel? If we are being honest, I think we'd agree that we could all benefit from seeing ourselves as our children see us. Children have a way of seeing into our hearts and souls. They don't judge us by out outer appearance as much as by the way we make them feel. I recently saw a quote by Lauren Jauregui, that I loved: "If only our eyes saw souls instead of bodies how very different our ideals of beauty would be."[35] Think about that for a minute. I believe that is what is meant when it tells us in the Bible to "be like a child."

If we could be like children and see like children again, we would more readily accept and believe the good things that others say and think about us.

Learn How to Accept a Compliment

When was the last time you got a sincere compliment?

If you are anything like the old me, you might struggle with accepting a compliment. When we can't find the goodness or worthiness in ourselves, it seems incredible that others could possibly see the good. It used to be that if people would tell me I looked good or was a good mom, I simply could not believe them because that was not what I believed about myself. I would deflect their compliments by saying something nice about them and getting the spotlight off of me. Or I would ignore them altogether or combat their nice comment with one that instantly deflated me again and made me feel normal.

Learning how to give and receive compliments is a great way to retrain the inner critic to work on our behalf and yield instant improvements in our lives. It takes practice, but within weeks of noticing our inner critics and replacing the words they say with better ones, we can see massive results in our self-confidence and acceptance. We will learn even more about that in the next chapter.

When you give your child a compliment, notice how they react. If they are still young enough, they will usually agree with you. You might say, "You are so good at coloring." And they will respond with "I know." Or we could say, "You are such a cutie pie," and they will agree.

Each of us is born with loads of confidence. When you think about a baby, you never think of someone who lacks confidence or self-love. Babies love and accept their bodies. They touch themselves and flaunt their nakedness without a care in the world. They aren't afraid to cry or laugh or express themselves, always knowing that they are loved and accepted. At what age does that change?

It seems that the ability to compare and feel less than is starting earlier and earlier. Kids are learning the art of body shaming and programming their inner critic at a much younger age. With so much screen time and parents that struggle with their own self-love, many kids are being raised and exposed to low-self-esteem as early as their preschool years. It was a very sad day for me when my preschooler came home and said she no longer wanted to wear her hair a certain way because the other kids made fun of it.

By learning to accept and give compliments to ourselves, our children, and even perfect strangers, we can instantly help everyone involved feel good. We can mimic the kind of behavior we want our children to maintain for as long as possible.

Know that if someone is saying something good about you, you are worthy of that praise. Just say, "thank you!" and believe them. It might make your day run smoother and make you feel great as well.

A Facebook Friends' conversation with her son:

"When my son was four, he noticed the varicose veins on my thigh. He asked me what they were, and I said, "Just some ugly veins mom has." He said, "I don't think they're ugly. I think it's cool my mom is camouflage!"

Give Compliments

Along with accepting compliments, you should try to give compliments to others as often as you can. It will attract more of them into your life. The more you give the more you will get back. If you think a good thought about someone else, share it.

I'm not sure why it is so hard for people to compliment each other. It sometimes seems like people would rather pull their own teeth out than say something genuinely nice to someone else. The more compliments you give, the happier it will make you and the more attractive you will become. When people feel good around you, they want to be around you. There is nothing quite as attractive as some good, old-fashioned kindness and praise toward another. If you want to feel good about yourself, try finding the good in others, tell them about it, and see how it makes you feel. I promise it will give you a little boost in your own self-esteem and more.

A simple, "You look good today" or "I love your hair" or "You have such a pretty smile" can literally brighten someone's entire day.

If you really want to make someone feel great, practice making your compliments even more grand. Rather than giving a simple compliment, if we make a point to go the extra mile with it, people will more readily believe what we are saying and what we say will not seem as trite.

Instead of saying, "You look good today" you could say, "You always look so good. I love that you take the time and attention to always make yourself look presentable and as pretty as possible. It inspires me to try harder."

Rather than saying to your child, "Good job on your homework" you could say, "I really appreciate how hard you work to get your homework done. You are so responsible and learning so well. I am very proud of you."

Watch what happens to their face when they see you have put some time and attention into the compliment. It makes you want to do it more!

Science also proves that giving a compliment to someone else helps you in several ways: "It takes the focus off of you. Smiling burns calories. Compliments spark creativity (remove mental blocks). Sincere compliments build trust (which earns you more friends and better relationships). And lastly, giving a compliment is *free*."[36] Giving at least one compliment daily can attract the loving relationships and friendships we seek in abundance. These relationships, thriving on positive energy, are among the top things on which a rich and fulfilling life is built.

You should start with the simple habit of giving yourself a compliment every single day and *talking to yourself like you would talk to your very own best friend*. Soon you will find that you *really are* your very own best friend and you won't need other people to be your cheerleaders or to compliment you for you to feel good about yourself. Such was the case for me.

This leads us to the next small but powerful step to easily improve your life: changing your words.

Chapter Highlights:

- Our inner critics come in many shapes and sizes, and they are unique for each of us. They target whatever it is that we secretly hate the most about ourselves, and feed on our fears.
- According to recent statistics, approximately 91% of women are unhappy with their bodies and resort to dieting. Only 5% of women naturally possess the body type often portrayed in the media.
- A recent survey shows that around 80% of Americans are not satisfied with their lives and really don't like their day jobs.
- Learning to retrain our inner critics to not only stop tearing our own life apart, but that of perfect strangers and good friends as well, isn't as hard as you might think.

- Rather than sizing others up to see how we are either better or worse than them, we can start looking for the good.
- You can make the choice right now, to become your own cheerleader and build yourself up rather than continue on the misery track.
- I now take full responsibility for the way I feel at all times. No one else has that power over me, and the same goes for you.
- You do not need to wait for a compliment from anyone but yourself. You can make yourself feel loved and appreciated, and you can do it at any time and in any place.
- Find out how you feel loved, then do those things for yourself.
- Learning how to give and receive compliments is a great way to retrain the inner critic to work on our behalf and yield instant improvements in our lives.
- By learning to accept and give compliments to ourselves, our children, and even perfect strangers, we can instantly help everyone involved feel good. We can mimic the kind of behavior we want our children to maintain for as long as possible.
- You should start with the simple habit of giving yourself a compliment every single day and talking to yourself like you would talk to your best friend.

Actions to Take:

1. Write down what are you most afraid of and why?

   _____

   _____

   _____

   _____

2. Are you currently satisfied with your life and your body? If not, what do you want to change and why?

   _____

   _____

   _____

   _____

3. Write down one compliment you can give your-self right now, then go and give someone else a compliment. How can you make this a daily habit?

   _____

   _____

   _____

   _____

4. Place your hand on your heart and repeat, "I am an amazing person. I am loved and needed."

HABIT FIVE:
CHANGE YOUR WORDS

"Words can inspire. And words can destroy.
Choose yours well."
—Robin Sharma

"You can change the course of your life
with your words."
—Anonymous

The Power of Words

I have no idea who coined the phrase, "Sticks and stones may break my bones, but words will never hurt me," but they weren't the shiniest coin in the bank. They must have been completely sheltered from the world, living with parents that only spoke in soft whispers and kind words, or maybe somewhere off in space.

Words can absolutely hurt us. They dig deep into the penetrating fibers of our subconscious mind and can stay there for an entire lifetime without being discovered. They have the power to change lives in a matter of seconds and to break even the strongest of men.

In Hebrews chapter 4 we read, "For the **word** of God is quick, and powerful, and sharper than a two-edged sword..."[37] Jesus proves that the word is more powerful than a very strong weapon. He also said, "By your words ye are justified and by your words ye are condemned."

By the power of words, wars can be won, hearts can be healed, and people can be converted.

I want you to imagine two scenarios for a moment, that will help highlight the power of a single solitary word.

First, you get a phone call about your spouse. You've been happily married for years and now you hear any of the following words, describing them or something they did—what is your reaction?

- Cancer
- Broke
- Fraud
- Dying
- Killed
- Affair

- Missing
- Fired

What emotions come to the surface as you ponder any of those scenarios?

Now, picture your best friend of many years calling and happily screaming into your ear:

- Engaged
- Pregnant
- Vacation
- Lottery-Winner
- Girls-Getaway
- So Happy!

Now how are you feeling?

These two scenarios paint completely different pictures on how a single word can instantly change our entire lives. Words have the power to cut like a knife and leave an impression on our psyche that can cause disease and despair, or confidence and joy.

For that reason, we must use extreme caution when speaking to ourselves and our little ones. Our inner critics are always there waiting in the shadows of our minds for the perfect or most inopportune time to pounce.

Teaching them a new vocabulary can yield real results quickly.

What kinds of words does your inner critic usually use? When you look at yourself in the mirror, what does it say? When you pass someone on the street who seems to have it all? When you browse through social media for hours on end?

Our subconscious mind retains everything we hear, see, feel, and think for our entire lifetime. It has file cabinets of stored information from every moment of our lives, ready for our inner critic to use as weapons against us at any time. This includes labels we were given when we were really young that somehow stuck (or that we might not even remember receiving). For this reason, we need to be extremely careful about the words we use to describe ourselves and our children.

What Labels Do You Have?

Think about your own childhood for a moment. Are there any words that were placed on you that stuck like permanent tattoos upon your mind and body? Were you labelled as being:

- Shy
- Lazy
- Worthless
- Annoying
- Short
- Tall
- Fat
- Ugly

Maybe you were given more positive labels such as:

- Smart
- Good
- Kind
- Gifted
- Beautiful
- Genius, etc.

Whatever the label that was placed upon you long ago, you can rewrite it and find a place within to erase your past, to delete the words your inner critic says and to rephrase them into things that your inner cheerleader can yell out in your time of need.

We tend to stick to the thoughts that are familiar to us. In fact, Dr. Joe Dispenza, a leading-edge scientist, says that 95% of our thoughts are the same thoughts that we had yesterday, meaning we only come up with new ideas and thoughts about five percent of the time. [38] What kind of thoughts are you unconsciously replaying in your mind from day to day? What kind do you play consciously?

A simple experiment with white rice can show you the results of what words can do to us physically. Cook some rice and divide it in half, putting each half in a separate mason jar with a lid. Then put a label on each jar, one getting something like "love" and the other getting "hate." Next you place each jar in a separate room and talk to each differently for about three weeks. Make sure the rooms aren't too close, so one jar can't hear the other jar's words. You only speak kind, loving words to the "love" jar, and hateful, unkind words and feelings towards the "hate" jar.

After three weeks of doing so a mysterious, yet amazing thing happens. The white rice in the love jar stays white, while the rice in the hate jar grows moldy and disgusting. Kids love this experiment.

A similar thing happens to water when frozen. A man by the name of Dr. Emoto took some samples of water on which different labels were placed. Some water molecules were labeled "love and thanks" while others had the words "I hate you, you make me sick" on them. He then froze the water molecules and took pictures of them. The "love and thanks" water formed beautiful crystal patterns, while the "hate" water turned to utter chaos. [39]

If this is happening to rice and water, what do you think might be happening to human beings? Especially since we are made of 70 percent water!

Changing the Vocabulary We Use

If you want to instantly impact your life for the good, you can start by changing the words you use every day. Let's experiment with a few common and familiar phrases that you could possibly be repeating every day both out loud and non-verbally. I want to show you the power of re-writing a single phrase, so you can see the difference it could make in your life.

Old Phrase	New Phrase
I don't have time	I can make time (if I want it bad enough)
This is overwhelming	This is thrilling
It's too hard	This is challenging but I can learn
Driving me crazy	This is pretty silly or helping me grow
I don't know	I can figure it out
Stressful	Testing me
I'm not in control	I am choosing this or I can gain control
I hate it	I don't love it but can learn something from this
I'm not worthy	I deserve this
I'll never be enough	I am always enough
I give up	Just keep swimming
I should	I could
It's impossible	I am possible or I can learn

What do you think would happen if we re-wrote the phrases and words that we used regularly in this way? The amazing personal development guru, Tony Robbins, says in his book, *Awaken the Giant Within*[40] that: "Simply by changing your habitual vocabulary—the words you consistently use to describe the emotions of your life—you can instantaneously change how you think, how you feel, and how you live." Then he gives an example of something that happened in his company that brought him and two of his other CEO's together to discuss a challenge they were having. He says the three men all used different words to describe their emotions (about the same situation), and their reactions were pretty much the same as the words they used. "…my CEO used "furious," "livid" and "enraged"; I called it "angry" or "upset"; and when it came to my friend, he poured his experience into the mold of "peeved" or "annoyed." What's interesting is that all of us, I discovered, use these same patterns of words to describe multitudes of frustrating experiences…. The words that we attach to our experiences become our experience… If we want to change our lives and shape our destiny, we need to consciously select the words we're going to use, and we need to constantly strive to expand our level of choice."

He goes on to describe how he decided to change his use of the words "angry" or "livid" with "peeved" and it made him smile. Using the silly word "peeved" made it that he wasn't as angry as he'd normally be in any given hard situation.

Four 4-Letter Words

In addition to the words and phrases on the chart, there are a few choice words that are overused and abused in our culture. It is time to either re-write them or abolish them from our vocabulary. It is no coincidence that they all have four letters, as we all know what the connotation behind four-letter-words is. They are killing our joy, minimizing our significance, and making us *feel* overwhelmed. Let's get rid of the following four-letter words:

1. **Busy**:

   How many times do you hear this word in a week? It has become all too common to use the word "busy" as an excuse. It almost seems like we think that being busy is a good thing, like a badge of honor. Being busy doesn't always mean productive, and it certainly doesn't equate to happiness. In fact, the busier we are, the more stressed we seem to be. Why not try to be less busy?

2. **Can't**:

   Too often we quit before we even get started because we feel that we can't do something. Maybe it is because we have tried in the past and failed. Perhaps it is due to the lack of knowledge or expertise. Whatever the excuse, let us acknowledge that that is exactly what we are doing: excusing ourselves from doing something or from not even trying to do something when we say we "cant" (minus the times we are using it to politely decline doing something we really cannot do). The only one saying we "can't" do something is ourselves (or someone else that has never done it before). Let's stop listening to that inner critic or that loudmouth know-it-all in our life that really doesn't know-it-all. If someone hasn't achieved what you are saying you can't do, you have no need to take advice from them!

Another thing that happens when we use the word "can't" is our mind instantly decides we shouldn't even try. Instead of saying "can't," what if we ask the simple question, "How can I?" When we do our subconscious goes to work for us and starts looking for ways that we can achieve what might otherwise seem impossible.

3. *Fine*:

When we are asked the common question, "How are you?" how many of us answer with the typical word, "fine?" Most of the time this word is a cop out for how we are *really* feeling. We are not "fine." We are stressed, tired, overwhelmed, frustrated, etc., yet we choose to portray ourselves as "fine." I have made it a rule to now change my response to that question. When someone asks me how I am feeling, I now try to answer with how I want to be feeling. I say, "fantastic," "great," "excited," etc. However, if I am having a particularly bad day, I express it and don't try to hide behind the word "fine." It's okay to own our feelings. Sometimes when we open up to others about the way we are feeling we are able to connect with them on a much deeper level.

4. *Just*:

This word has become a filler and a nuisance. How many times have you heard a mother say,

"I'm *just* a mom."? Or "I'm *just* a teacher/secre-tary/nurse/etc.? It's ridiculous. Why do we feel the need to downplay who we are? Why is there a tendency for us women to feel like we are less than or not good enough to simply be "a mom" instead of "*just* a mom?" (or whatever is it that you feel you are "just___"). In my opinion, this word should be deleted from our vocabulary altogether. It is not needed.

Marisa Peer, a famous life coach and hypnotherapist says, "The words you use form your reality. Change the words you use and change your reality. The words we use are often associated with pictures in our sub-conscious mind. We can see a butterfly vs. a moth; a caterpillar vs. a worm; the worst-case scenario or the best."[41]

Dr. Joe Dispenza says, "Your thoughts form your personality. Change your thoughts and change your personal reality."[42]

If you don't currently love your personal reality or the way you feel about yourself, it is time to start re-writing the way you talk to yourself and about your-self. In order to do this, you'll need to become a bit of a spy. You'll need to spend some time evaluating yourself and how you think and feel.

Spy on Yourself and Take Notes

As you go about your day, I want you to become more aware of your inner critic and start to recognize the words that you frequently use. This is a great way to become more mindful and to see how much you have been listening to this nasty voice rather than feeding your inner cheerleader. Write down or pay attention to how many times this inner critic is speaking to you and what it is saying. The goal is to become so aware of the negative thoughts, that you can starve them to death. As a food critic can't complain about food he hasn't eaten; your inner critic will have nothing to say to you if you stop feeding it and caring about what it says.

Throughout your day I want you to listen to the voices in your head in a different kind of way. Instead of caring about what they say, I want you to stand by like a third-party observer and write down what they are saying without any judgement or thought. At the end of the day write down how much or how little you noticed, record the thoughts and feelings you had while observing, and write down anything new that you learned from this experiment. (I will be covering how to re-write these phrases in the next chapter).

_____

_____

_____

_____

Self-observation and evaluation is a great way to start improving your life and re-writing your story.

By changing simple words and phrases in our vocabulary, we can add more joy and satisfaction to our lives and to motherhood.

One word that I think many mothers need to learn to use a lot more is "*no*" (and I'm not referring to using it more with your children).

Just Say, "No!"

A lot of my fellow mom friends are overextending themselves to the point where they regularly feel stressed.

They are involved in multiple volunteer opportunities through work, school, community, or church, and as a result they are often frazzled and overwhelmed. When I ask them how they got to be so involved and if they like it, they always say: "I was asked to and couldn't say *no*," or, "so-and-so needed my help and I just couldn't tell her *no*."

Learning the art of saying *no* is a great way to de-stress your life and give yourself a break. There is a time and a place for everything, and sometimes the things you will be asked to do won't be especially meaningful and exciting for you to do. At those times, it is absolutely okay to say something like, "Sorry, I can't do that right now."

Do you find yourself saying *"yes"* to things that you hate doing or have no desire to do? If so, changing even a few of your *"yes's"* to *"no's"* can help you out in a big way.

Something that has helped me know when to say *"yes"* versus *"no"* is to have a personal mission statement of intention. I think about what I really want out of my life in any given time or stage, then I write an overarching statement of intention of how I'm going to achieve those things that I want. I will get more into this in the chapter about goals, but for now, let's use it to learn how to say *"no."*

For the past year I have used the following mission statement: "I desire more than anything else, to awaken as many people as I can to the potential they have within; to inspire them to live a life they love—to love themselves, their neighbors, and their lives, to the point where every single day feels like Christmas! I want to help countless people emotionally, spiritually, and financially. I want to be financially free to help and inspire people every day!"

When I am asked to do something, I can ask myself if this situation will align with my major goals or intentions, or if it will take me on a detour. This helps when I get conflicted on how to spend my time. If I'm asked to go somewhere or volunteer for something or do anything, I immediately ask, "Will this help me inspire and awaken others to their potential... etc. or will it simply take time away from the things that are more important?" If it appears to be taking me on a detour, I have no problem saying no.

If you struggle with saying *no*, recognize that you can't keep saying *yes* and be true to who you really want to be. Eventually you will get burned out and want to say no to everything. I have become really good at saying no, so much so that sometimes I feel guilty not helping out. However, when I weigh the purpose of volunteering up against why I am saying *no*, I always feel better.

For example, I used to be involved in the PTO at school and helped out with fundraisers and other things. This year, I have only been to one meeting. I know that there are other moms to help out (thank you so much you wonderful women!), and I have this deeper need to spend my time writing this book (knowing that eventually this book will help so many more people than I could ever serve by volunteering at an elementary school). I will go back and serve them when I feel like it aligns with my main objectives and goals again, but for now, I am serving a different need.

Sometimes your goal might simply be to *stay happy or afloat*. Many women do not dream quite as big as me and that is perfectly fine. Your biggest goal or mission statement could be as simple as "be the best mom I can be." We all know that motherhood is one of the hardest jobs on the planet, and that no mother has it all together all of the time. Becoming the best at motherhood that you can is a very noble and wonderful goal to have. If that is the case, then you can allow yourself to say *yes* to the things that will align with that. Just be careful not to overdo it and feel like you have to be a "Pinterest-worthy" mom at all times.

If you know that volunteering to be the homeroom mom for your kid's class or being in charge of the local 4H Club (or whatever it is that is beckoning for your time) is going to place a burden on your already overloaded schedule, do yourself a favor and *say no*! You'll prevent yourself from running out of gas and you'll show yourself more love and respect by doing so. You will free up time to do the things that really matter to you and to be with the ones you love.

Just Say, "Please?"

Most mothers have very giving hearts and positive intentions. But sometimes our kindness backfires. Sometimes it stresses us out. Sometimes we get taken advantage of or misused (which is why I caution you to say *no*). Another thing we can learn to do in addition to saying *no*, is to simply **ask for help!** I know, for some of you that seems even worse than being overwhelmed with having too much on our plate, but trust me, it can be a lifesaver (or at least a stress-reliever!).

Often, we have a tendency to feel like we not only can, but should, take everything on *all by ourselves*. That is a lead contributor to much of our stress. So many of us hate to ask for help. Maybe it's the idea of admitting we don't have it all together. Maybe we feel it is a sign of weakness or failure, but friend, let me assure you that it is not! Learning to ask for help can alleviate our stress, give those that help us an opportunity to serve (which makes them feel good), and get the job done in a lot less time or effort. Sounds like a win-win, right?

The next time you are trying to make dinner while holding a screaming baby, talking to some underpaid telecommunications person on the phone about a bill, while your husband sits on the couch reading a book-*ask him **out loud** for help*! I have learned that most men don't see our craziness and unless we *open our mouths and ask them specifically* to "come take the baby" or "stir this sauce," etc. they usually won't even notice our impending meltdown. No matter how obvious our dilemma might seem to us, other people *cannot read our minds.* If we don't speak up, it can lead us to build-up resentment towards them. Prevent such feelings by **asking for help!** And don't forget to use the word, "please."

If you have overbooked yourself again and have three places to be at the same time and no way to clone yourself, is there a friend you can call for help? What I have found is that most women, especially our friends, will drop what they are doing and come to our aid, *if* we ask them too. Service for another makes us feel good. Sometimes asking for help is the best way you can serve others. It can also be the best way to prevent an anxiety or stress-induced health problem! *Side-note: when we are having a particularly bad day or feeling down, one of the fastest ways to pick-ourselves-back-up is to serve someone else.

In addition to changing our vocabulary, it is also important to be aware of our expectations, interpretations, and our bad habits.

"The difference between successful people and very successful people is that very successful people say 'no' to almost everything."
—Warren Buffet

What Do You Expect?

Too many of us expect perfection out of ourselves. We write a big to-do list, only to feel like a failure at the end of the day if we have not crossed everything off. We expect ourselves to be able to handle every disappointment and interruption of the day without preparing for them, and we set ourselves up for failure by doing this. We want to be the "perfect" wife and mother. We want to look good, have the perfect body, keep a clean and orderly home, take care of the kids and get them where they need to be, have a delicious meal on the table, and never raise our voices. We all seem to be under the impression that we need to be "perfect." But what does that even mean?

"Perfect" is another word that we need to re-write.

If you've ever heard the phrase from scripture, "Be ye therefore perfect, even as your Father which is in heaven is perfect"[43] you might feel a little guilty. Sometimes when we read scriptures or go to church, we are bombarded with feelings of inadequacy or shame. Other times we experience similar feelings when comparing ourselves to what appear to be "better" mothers than us. We feel like we are not "good enough", not "doing it right," or like we are "failing" as moms. If we expect ourselves to be as "perfect" as our Father in Heaven, we are setting ourselves up for failure. It might help you to know what Jesus really meant when he said that phrase.

When I really want to understand the context and true meaning behind words and phrases in the scriptures, I like to look in *Strongs Concordance*[44]. It gives us the Hebrew or Greek definition for the words used back in Biblical times. When I looked up the word "perfect" it surprised me. It didn't say "doing everything right all the time and always obeying the commandments." Instead, it said that perfect meant, "finished or complete." I thought that was pretty profound. We don't have to be just like God, we just need Him to help us be complete. Perhaps this knowledge can help alleviate some of your mom guilt or feelings of inadequacy.

It is overwhelming and impossible to be what the "world" thinks of as "perfect." Granted, there are some women who appear to have it all: a fantastic career, a husband with a great job, the "perfect" body/house/car/kids, etc. (especially if we only observe these things on social media!). We can get caught up in trying to keep up with what others think is the "perfect life."

However, perfection is completely based on opinion and perspective. It's subjective. Each of us have different backgrounds and abilities and see things in diverse ways. What would be considered the perfect man to one woman would not be anything near what another woman might want. Some may say, "That is the perfect house," while others would not agree, seeing it as too big, too small, too boxy, etc.

We each come with our own unique vantage point and background that we use as a filter to define our particular view of "perfection." It's a good thing that we all have different desires, tastes, and things we love. If we all wanted the same thing and thought that there really was only one true idea or way of being perfect, the world would be boring and probably even more competitive and comparative than it is today. Remember the saying, "One man's trash is another man's treasure"? What makes this so? It is the background or lens through which each man is looking at life.

When we put pressure on ourselves, our husband, or our children to be "perfect," we are only setting ourselves up for disappointment and piling on more mom guilt. We will never be happy if our expectations are too high. We can prevent such an outcome by simply lowering our expectations and letting things go.

Instead of expecting everything to be *perfect* all the time, why not try to let go of the reigns and just enjoy or deal with things as they come?

Let Go

Another often misunderstood phrase from the Bible is, "be still." Often, we interpret them to mean, "be reverent," or "don't move or make a noise." Again, what I found in *Strongs Concordance*[45], might surprise you. The word "still" means "go, leave, or weaken." Today we could use the common phrase, "let it go" to define "be still." This new interpretation just might be the antidote to many of the stresses and guilt we feel so often as mothers.

"Be still" or "let it go" in modern-day vernacular, means stop stressing about all the little things that happen. Let the spilled milk just be spilled milk, not a reason to get angry or to yell. Let the mud on the floor you just mopped be a lesson for a child to pick up after themselves and not for us to muddy our attitude. When the dishes break, remember that the precious soul who broke them is more important than the dish itself. When our husband can't seem to read our mind and do what we want him to do without us having to ask, can we just give him the benefit of the doubt and realize that he is not a mind reader? When the dishes or clothes aren't put away in the exact way that we desire, is it possible for us to just "be still" about it? Can we "weaken" our control and proclaim, "It is what is it"?

Maybe what we really need to let go of are things from our past. Perhaps we need to forgive someone. Maybe even ourselves. Forgiveness can be a powerful way to heal our pain and increase our joy. Instead of saying, "I should have," "I shouldn't have," "I wish I would have," "I can't believe I," "if only," etc., we can simply choose to let those things go. What if we give ourselves some credit, and let those "bad" things from our past be the stepping stones that made us who we are today? Dwelling in the past is not doing anything good for the present. Neither is allowing mistakes, or negative words, to take over our minds and our moods.

I know that this is a lot easier said than done. I am nowhere near "perfect" when it comes to letting it go. Just now, as I finished writing the words above, I was bombarded with feelings of inadequacy and like I am a hypocrite. I got angry with my husband for not doing something I wanted from him and was tempted to yell at my kids. Recognizing these feelings made me feel guilty, and the snow ball started. I felt like an imposter. How could I possibly write a book about a message I wasn't living?

However, rather than losing control, punching someone in the face, or pulling my hair out, I went into another room, cuddled up with a blanket and evaluated myself. It dawned on me that my hormones were out of whack (which is totally normal the week before "Aunt Flo" comes to visit). I realized that no one reading this book expects me to be perfect and that no mom has it all together 100 percent of the time. I recognized that although I might know the answers, it isn't always easy to live them. Immediately I felt peace. I gave myself a break, and a hug. Instead of beating myself up for not living up to my own expectations, I am choosing to show myself some compassion and love. We are all works in progress. *Knowing what to do is only part of the battle.*

Lower Your Expectations

Did you notice how I said I didn't live up to *my own expectations*? Expectations can be some of the most stress-inducing things that we have. They are behind the majority of our struggles and the reason why so many of us are feeling like failures.

Knowing what we should do or what is expected of us doesn't always motivate or help us achieve it. Understanding this concept can help us in our relationships. Just because our kids, partners, or coworkers know something is the "right thing to do" or will make *you* happy (not necessarily them), doesn't always mean they will do it. Sometimes we actually <u>expect too much of them</u> and it can backfire.

I am in no way insinuating that we need to have zero expectations. In many areas we must have high standards for our kids, ourselves, and our partners. We should expect our husband to be loyal, our kids to do their best at school, be respectful and kind, and ourselves to try our hardest, etc. However, we need to be careful with how high those standards are, and that they are not based on our own need to be in control.

If we expect our kids to get straight A's and they occasionally don't, it can end up hurting them more than helping. I learned this the hard way when one of my daughters was scared to death to show me her report card. She hid it from me, lied that she had lost it, and then cried her eyes out before revealing her grades. By the way she was reacting, I thought that she had flunked out of 3rd grade, but instead was shocked that she was losing it over a B+. It was a big wakeup call to me. I cried with her and made sure she knew that she was so much more than her grades and that they did not determine who she was or how smart she was. I reminded her that often those that don't graduate the head of their class turn out to be the most successful in life. Grades don't determine our worth.

I realized that by putting that much pressure on my kids to excel in school and get all A's, I was inadvertently making this sweet daughter feel like she wasn't good enough or smart enough. I was making her afraid of me. That was the last thing I wanted, and I have since learned to loosen my expectations. Instead of saying they must get all A's, I ask my kids if they are doing their absolute best. I have learned that they don't get as resentful or scared when they know that I won't blow up at them (yes, I have done that in the past) for not performing up to *my standards.* Just because I had straight A's in school doesn't mean that everyone I raise can or should!

Forcing others to do things often makes them resentful and brings up negative feelings towards those things in the future. I know of ton of teenagers and young adults that leave the churches they were raised in because they were forced to do/not do things. I know many adults that hate a certain food or exercise because they were made to eat it or do it when they were younger. So many people build up emotional walls to things that they are *forced* against their will to do. Most of these are based on a parent's desire to make sure that their kids "turn out alright." They are *based on love* but sometimes come off to the child as *anything but love.* It is more beneficial for them to be given a soft choice rather than forcing them to do something. It is better to celebrate their efforts rather than bash them for not doing something perfectly.

For example, I expect my husband and kids to wash dishes, replace toilet paper when it runs out, and to put away their laundry. Let's say they did the dishes, but they weren't put in the dishwasher the same way I would have done it (this is a common problem for many women). Can we choose to rejoice that the job got done, and see that the dishes are still clean, even if it wasn't the way "it should have been done?" ie: the way we *preferred* it?

The same goes for laundry. I have seen marriages end because a wife couldn't handle the fact that her husband wouldn't put his clothes away *"the right way."* Just because it is the way *you do it*, doesn't mean it is the *right* way, it's just the way you *prefer* it. There are many ways of going about our duties and getting them done. So long as the job gets done, we should celebrate it a success. Control makes us feel horrible when it is not followed and can distance us from the ones we are trying to control (even if it is done out of love.)

By lowering our expectations of ourselves, our schools, our children, and other people, we can instantly free ourselves from the victim mentality and allow greater love into our lives. Our families will feel so much happier when can stop tethering them to an expectation that is set so high that they cannot reach it. When we cut ourselves and others loose from the bands of perfection or control, all will feel lighter, more relaxed, less stressed, and less guilty. How's that for a change of vocabulary? What mom wouldn't choose "relaxed" over "stressed"?

Simply changing the word "expect" to "prefer" in our minds, will help alleviate a lot of our struggles.

Again, it is easier said than done. I still struggle with it, even after seeing its magical effects on my life. But when we have the right tools, everything becomes so much easier to do. Little by little, we catch ourselves in the act of feeling sorry for ourselves, or repeating old limiting beliefs, or expecting too much, and we slowly sharpen our awareness and progress.

Another tool to add to your motherhood toolbox is the art of not complaining. Using different vocabulary and ways to describe what we are experiencing can absolutely make motherhood and life more enjoyable.

Do You Have the Bad Habit of Complaining?

For years I was in the bad habit of expressing my negative thoughts about all of the things that happened in my life. I would tell the same sob stories over and over, as if they were making me look or sound good. It never solved anything. I guess it was yet another way of seeking attention or approval. I would wait for my husband to get home so that I could rattle off a laundry list of complaints almost daily. It was routine that as soon as he walked in the door, he was greeted with something like this:

"I had the worst day. I had to change 13 diapers, the kids got poop all over my new shirt. I burned dinner because the baby threw up all over the couch. I didn't get the laundry done, I have such a bad headache, etc. etc. etc."

I don't know of anyone who likes coming home to someone who has nothing good to say. No one looks forward to walking in the door and hearing someone whine and complain. I had no idea what kind of burden greeting him with complaints put on my poor husband, but I know we are both grateful that I grew out of those bad habits and learned a better way.

Now, when my husband walks in the door after working all day, I make it a point to be positive and focus on the good things that happened in my day. I greet him with a smile and a hug, and I focus on meeting his needs rather than selfishly expressing all of mine. He in turn, rarely (if ever) complains about his day. He leaves his worries or concerns at work. This gives us the time and energy to spend uplifting each other and having quality time together as a family. We still have our bad days, but we choose to focus on the positive within them and try our best to see the good in all things.

At this point you might be asking, "But how can I stop complaining?" Here are a few tips that I have learned to change my bad habit into a better one:

1. **Become more aware** of when you are complaining. The first step to fixing a problem, is recognizing you have one. (The inner critic and complainer are siblings and go hand-in-hand).

2. **Realize** that by talking, complaining, or giving your attention to things you don't want, you are only welcoming more of that negativity into your life. Stop giving the bad things your energy!

3. **Write** all the things you feel and think about a situation on a piece of paper. Get all those thoughts and feelings out of your body. Then throw the paper away, bury it, burn it or do something to forget about it. This gets all the negative emotion out of your body.

4. **Think** about the ill effects of complaining. You don't want to be the kind of person other people want to avoid. You also don't want to make their day worse. When you complain to others

it creates more negativity or worry in their lives and it isn't worth it.

5. **Complain to a higher power.** I pray and get all my frustrations out with the Almighty. He can fix things a lot easier than I can. Asking Him what lesson you can learn from whatever it is you are complaining about will often bring clarity.

6. **Start counting your blessings.** This goes back to the first and most important habit I talked about in this book: gratitude. When we start noticing ourselves complaining, we can change our mood by simply changing the way we are thinking and expressing ourselves.

7. **Recognize that complaining about something never solves the problem,** it usually makes it worse.

Oftentimes I will hear people say, "I'm not complaining... but_____." When you put that "but" in the sentence, you really are complaining; just admit it, then stop it! Try and re-write whatever you were going to say before you even say it.

By changing the words or phrases we use, lowering our expectations and avoiding complaining, we will find ourselves feeling happier and healthier in no time. This habit will take a little bit of effort and super-sleuthing on your part, but you will reap the rewards in no time.

Now that you are more aware of some of the words and phrases you (or your inner critic) use regularly, you are ready to move on and learn how to re-write them. By the end of the next chapter, you will be able to not only think differently, but your self-talk will transform as well. What do you currently say to yourself when you pass by or look into a mirror? Let's explore this together in the next chapter.

Chapter Highlights:

- Words can absolutely hurt us. They dig deep into the penetrating fibers of our subconscious mind and can stay there for an entire lifetime without being discovered. They have the power to change lives in a matter of seconds and to break even the strongest of men.

- Our subconscious mind retains everything we hear, see, feel, and think for our entire lifetime. It has file cabinets of stored information from every moment of our lives, ready for our inner critic to use as weapons against us at any time.

- Whatever the label that was placed upon you long ago, you can rewrite it and find a place within to erase your past, to delete the words your inner critic says and to rephrase them into things that your inner cheerleader can yell out in your time of need.

- 95% of our thoughts are the same thoughts that we had yesterday, meaning we only come up with new ideas and thoughts about five percent of the time.

- Both white rice and water react to the labels they are given. If that is the case, what do you think happens to human beings?

- If you want to instantly impact your life for the good, you can start by changing the words you use every day.

- "The words you use form your reality. Change the words you use and change your reality."
- Remember the 4-letter words!
- Do you find yourself saying "yes" to things that you hate doing or have no desire to do? If so, changing even a few of your "*yes's*" to "*no's*" can help you out in a big way.
- "Perfect" is another word that we need to re-write.
- Perfection is completely subjective. Each of us have different backgrounds and abilities and see things in diverse ways. What would be considered the perfect man to one woman would not be anything near what another woman might want.
- We will never be happy if our expectations are too high.
- Learning to say *no* and *please* can alleviate a lot of our stressors as mothers.
- Too many of us spend a lot of time complaining and focusing on the negative. Complaining about something never makes it better. It wastes our energy and makes us a harder person to be around.

Actions to Take:

Write down your answers to the following questions:

1. What kinds of words does your inner critic usually use? When you look at yourself in the mirror, what does it say? When you pass someone on the street who seems to have it all? When you browse through social media for hours on end?

   _____

   _____

   _____

   _____

2. What labels were you given in childhood?

   _____

   _____

   _____

   _____

3. Take a few minutes to write down your own personal mission statement: (start by thinking of what it is that you really want the most and what you will or will not do to achieve it.)

   _____

   _____

   _____

   _____

4. Start saying *yes* only to the things that will align with your new mission statement.

5. Write a list of people that you could ask for help if you were to need it, and then use it when you are feeling overwhelmed.

6. What kind of expectations are you placing on yourself or others? Do you need to lower those expectations? How can you do that starting today?

_____

_____

_____

_____

7. Are you in the habit of complaining? What action can you take today to become more aware of your habit and change your vocabulary?

_____

_____

_____

_____

8. Place your hand on your heart and repeat out loud, "I don't need to be perfect. I can let things go. I am strong enough to change my words and to know when to say *no* and when to ask for help."

HABIT SIX:
START SEEING YOURSELF FOR WHO YOU REALLY ARE

"You are loved. Massively. Ferociously. Unconditionally. The Universe is totally freaking out about how awesome you are. It's got you wrapped in a warm gorilla hug of adoration. It wants to give you everything you desire. It wants you to be happy. It wants you to see what it sees in you."

—Jen Sincero,
You Are A Badass

"Dear self: It's a shame how hard you are on yourself. You treat others with more love than you treat you. You deserve to be celebrated too."

—Anonymous

Mirror Work

The late Louise Hay, a wonderful coach and teacher about how to love yourself developed a program she called *Mirror Work*, that is simple yet profound. She tells us to look ourselves in the eye in front of a mirror and observe what we see and feel when we say the words, "I love you and accept you exactly the way you are."[46] She taught seminars and workshops worldwide in which she had her attendees' practice this in front of a mirror and then got their reactions. She would then respond to them, helping them overcome the emotional and deep-rooted limiting beliefs they held about themselves.

Some would say that saying they loved themselves in the mirror made them feel extremely uncomfortable, like they were lying. Others would feel pathetic and fearful. Some might feel guilt or resentment, allowing their inner critics to beat them up over daring to say such a thing. Louise calmly led each of her followers to a better self-image and life by simply having them repeat this phrase over and over every time they saw a mirror for the next few weeks.

It is amazing how quickly the unfamiliar becomes familiar and acceptable with constant repetition.

I personally tried this technique and found it to work wonders for me. For years I avoided looking in the mirror and only did it for as long as absolutely necessary to try to make myself look presentable. I loathed my body, found my hair to be atrocious, and felt uncomfortable making eye contact with myself and anyone else. After simply looking in every mirror I passed and saying that I loved and accepted myself, I was able to experience true self-love and transformation in very little time. It seems that the more we repeat things, the more our subconscious can grab ahold of them and make them a part of us. If we want those things to be good, we need to focus on the good and repeat the things that we want to believe over and over. When we hear the bad inner critic trying to take over, we can stop it in its tracks before it gains any momentum. Repetition is key in learning a new vocabulary.

Brian Tracy, another multi-millionaire speaker, author, and coach does something very similar. He teaches people in his book, *Million Dollar Habits*, to walk around all day saying, "I like myself"[47] over and over.

Lily: "MOM"

Me: "Yes, honey?"

Lily: "NO, it's not honey, it's Lily."

You Are Enough

Another simple thing that we can do with our mirrors is write the phrase, "I am enough" on them with a dry erase marker. The simple act of reading that phrase every time we wash our hands, brush our teeth, or pass by, leaves its mark on our subconscious mind and helps us to begin believing we are worthy and enough. My husband and I prefer to write, "I am more than enough" as it feels less limiting. Marisa Peer has said, "The easiest and fastest way to gain self-esteem is self-praise." She also says, "The root cause behind every issue is an issue of self-confidence or self-love." [48]

I have felt that way for a long time. In today's medical practices we are often addressing the symptoms of an issue without addressing the root cause. While that might take away our pain in the short term, the pain and disease will always return until we address its source.

By making eye contact with our inner child and praising ourselves or telling ourselves that we are enough or loved, we can heal a lifetime of pain and insecurity in a matter of days.

The biggest hurdle in doing this is that many people simply do not believe that they are enough. They have been programmed to believe that they have to earn their worthiness and prove their "enoughness." This is simply not true. We are all intrinsically enough all of the time.

We do not need to be homeroom mom or bring Pinterest-worthy treats to school for our kids to think that we are enough. We don't have to be the most fit and strong mom to feel like we are good enough. We don't even have to shower regularly or put on makeup or even get out of our pajamas to be good enough. We are always enough, and we are exactly what our kids need.

However, being raised in a culture that seems to encourage shaming ourselves and proving our rightness, goodness, fitness level, and expertise, it is no wonder why so many of us struggle with feeling like we are worthy. We feel like we have to make the grade, prove our ability, or do everything right to earn our worthiness. Is it possible that we have been lying to ourselves?

The parable of the prodigal son in the Bible[49] helps to prove my point. There was a rich father who had two sons. He planned on giving them both an inheritance, but the younger more rebellious son didn't want to wait to get his. He wanted to be free and live the life that he desired. He asked, and his father gave him his inheritance early. Then the young son took his inheritance and lived a "life of sin" and squandered away every single bit of that inheritance. His father anxiously waited for this son to return, day after day, concerned for his safety and well-being. One day the boy finally did return. His father was overjoyed and had the fatted calf (luxury) killed for a feast in the son's honor. Never once did the father make this young son feel like he wasn't "worthy" or enough. He didn't cast him out for being wasteful and making mistakes. He loved him unconditionally and yearned only for his happiness and return.

In the eyes of God, we are all worthy all of the time. Worth doesn't change because we sin or make mistakes. We never have to earn our value or prove ourselves to Him. He loves us without conditions all the time.

As a mother, I can completely understand how this father must have felt and am learning more and more about how God really feels about us, His children. If I were to have to watch my children make bad choices and waste their talents, time, or money on things that I found to be "bad" it might break my heart, but it would never make me question their worth. They would always be worthy of my love and adoration. I would always love them, and care for them, and want what is best for them.

The same goes for a dollar bill, a $20, or any cash for that matter. Even the most beat-up, weathered and abused bills are still worth the full amount of their value. Just because they've been written on, made dirty, used in the wrong way, or mistreated, doesn't make a dollar any less than a dollar. It is worth its full value regardless of what has happened in its past or what it might be used for.

Learning that you are enough all of the time is crucial to your overall happiness. You don't need to prove your value to anyone but yourself. Let me assure you—YOU ARE ENOUGH and YOU ARE WORTHY! You can come to believe that yourself in very little time with mirror work and writing "I am enough" on your mirror.

There is one more thing that we can do in front of our mirrors to help reprogram our subconscious mind. This technique really teaches our inner cheerleader how to shine. It is called "doing affirmations."

What is an Affirmation?

To affirm something means to "state or assert positively or maintain as true." When we are feeling low, we can talk ourselves out of that feeling and choose to focus on something that we really want to feel. When we fake it long enough, we will in time begin to believe it and then feel it. It is akin to what I heard a music teacher tell her students who were about to go on stage: "If you don't feel good or peppy, if you feel scared or unsure of yourself, remember you are a performer. Performers can fake it under the worst of circumstances- they get by with a smile on their face, even if they feel like their world is falling apart. Fake it 'til you make it."

When we want to become better at something, or we want to debunk the junk in our mind and get on a new track of thinking, we should affirm that we can. By repeating certain phrases or mantras, we can reprogram the way we think and feel and help rewire our brains. It's like giving our computer an overhaul and deleting its cookies and cache so that we can start fresh and perform better.

Daily affirmations have become a way of boosting my morale and making myself feel better. These can be short and sweet or long and flowery. You can pick whatever it is that will make you feel good. I chose a few things that I really wanted to believe about myself. In addition to the phrases that I already mentioned, we can make our own.

When we say things over and over each day, with *feeling* while we look in the mirror, we start to change our own minds and begin believing them. It can feel really cheesy and awkward for the first week or so, but it is so worth it. It's wonderful when we start believing ourselves and can actually look at the mirror and take ourselves seriously.

Whether we know it or not, every day we are proclaiming affirmations to the universe that affect who we are and what we feel. We do this all day every day. Whenever we use the words, "I AM" together, we create powerful scenarios and beliefs in our minds.

Think about what words we usually put after that small phrase.

- "I am lonely."
- "I am sad." "
- I am pathetic."
- "I am tired."
- "I am sick."
- "I am desperate."
- "I am fat."
- "I am ugly." etc.

Each time we use those phrases we place another label or sticker on our subconscious mind, increasing its impact and intensity in our soul. The words we use are a lot more powerful than we often think. Even the smallest drop of water, if allowed to continue dripping, can make a huge dent in what seems a permanent condition. Repetition is key.

Doing affirmations is another way to re-write the vocabulary used by our inner critics.

To make affirmations work in our favor, we need to become aware of when we say them (mindful of the inner critic) and we need to rehearse and practice using new more empowering phrases. I had you write down the words of your inner critic in the last chapter, but I'm going to help you re-write them now. I want to help you change them into powerful statements that can transform your beliefs about yourself.

When I started using affirmations, I desperately wanted to learn to love myself, more specifically my body. I had been on diet after diet and after many years had finally hit my goal weight. It should have been a powerfully victorious moment in my life, but instead it was a defining moment. It was upon looking in the mirror after years of working towards the goal I had achieved that my personal development journey began.

Instead of feeling on top of the world and hugely proud of myself, I noticed that I still looked fat. I still saw my lack of a six-pack and my nothingness. It was shocking. I truly had believed for so long that if I got back to my pre-pregnancy size I would finally be happy and confident in my body. That was not the case.

Realizing then that happiness wasn't to be found in a pants size, I started searching for real and lasting change. It was then that I came upon affirmations. I cannot remember how I got started with them, but I know that they work. That year I made the New Year's resolution to "learn to love myself no matter my size" and I was determined to keep it. One of the easiest and fastest ways I was able to achieve that goal was to use affirmations in the mirror.

I started with phrases like:

- "I am worth it."
- "I love you; I really, really love you!"
- "I am beautiful."

- "God loves me, and I do too."
- "I can do all things with Christ, who strengthens me."

Over time I began to believe these things and found that saying them to myself was just as good, if not better than hearing them from other people. I found that I could be my own cheerleader, my own support group, and my own best friend! I was shocked when I started to look in the mirror with a smile and really feel that I was telling myself the truth. It was both empowering and fun. I have now advanced to performing full-blown coaching sessions with myself in front of the mirror and find that I always feel better after giving myself a pep-talk.

After a while you will find that the affirmations become second nature. You might even get to the point where you believe them so much you don't even need to say them anymore. Then you can choose new things to affirm in your mind, as we are always trying to advance and become more. We will never stop progressing, learning, and refining ourselves. Our daily affirmations need never become commonplace or boring. We can change them as we change.

A Facebook Friend of mine and her 3-year-old:

Z: "Mom, I love you."
Mom: "I love you too, sweetie."
Z: "You're my favorite mom in the whole world."
Mom: "You're my favorite 3-year-old in the whole world."
Z: "You are beautiful!"
Mom: "Awww..." (then she interrupted me...)
Z: "Not as beautiful as me, but still beautiful."
Mom: I laughed out loud.

How to Write an Affirmation

I know it seems very elementary to teach you how to write an affirmation, but when I started doing it, I learned I was doing it wrong and I don't want you to make the same mistake. First, you need to take baby steps to where you want to be. Your subconscious mind will reject affirmations that are so far from what you currently feel that you cringe or don't believe a word you say. You need to find things that are slightly more believable than something that feels too "out there." Training our mind to believe these affirmations is like anything else, you start small then build on it.

If you really can't stand your body and start saying, "I love my body" your conscious mind will automatically reject that idea and it will not even come close to letting your subconscious mind hear it. Instead you need to start by saying something like:

- "I am open to the idea of loving my body regardless of how much I weigh."
- "I desire to feel great love for my body."
- "I am grateful for all that I do love about my body."
- "I am a work in progress and getting better every day."
- "I have an open mind to accept good things about myself."
- "I am learning to love and accept my body."

These kinds of phrases will ease you into believing the more "hard-core" beliefs, like "I love my body just the way it is." "I am perfect the way I am." Your subconscious mind will only start believing what you are saying and allow you to make the positive changes, when you *feel* it is real. Your emotions about what you are saying have a ton to do with how much you will absorb and allow it to change you. When you say things long enough and with an open heart, eventually you will begin to believe them. Start with believable phrases that will stretch you a little in the right direction, then add to them as you go.

Keep it Positive

Another important tip is only using positive words in your affirmations. When I first started, I would say things like: "I am debt free." "I can lose weight." "I am not fat." These don't sound wrong, do they? Well, they are. Let me explain:

The first thing to do is decide what you want. Once you decide what you desire more than anything else (love, riches, health, happiness, etc.) or a combination of them all, you can start writing positive affirmations about them. To do that, you must take any negative words out of the phrase and replace them with their positive opposite. This is crucial because your subconscious mind cannot take a joke. It takes you completely literally 100% of the time. That means that even when you say things in jest, you are creating a vibration that your subconscious mind thinks *is totally serious.*[50]

For example, when you want to lose weight, do not say, as in my example above: "I am not fat." "I can lose weight." The words "not, don't and lose" are all negative and do not convey the real end goal to your mind.

Instead, you should say, "I have perfect health. I am the perfect size." "I weigh 130 lbs. or (260 lbs. of pure muscle if you're like my husband)." "I have six pack abs." You want to use words and phrases that convey that you have already met the goal and really feel it.

If you want wealth, use words like, "I am financially free." NOT "I am debt free." When you exchange the word "debt" with something like freedom, you focus on the good feeling not the bad. This is because our subconscious mind works in images. Whatever picture comes to the mind with certain words is what it will focus on. So, by saying the words "debt," "fat," "not," etc. our minds will see the pictures of those things.

Write what you want specifically, "I make a million dollars a year." Not "I have more money." Notice how I put a time frame (but not a deadline) on when to become a millionaire- if not you could wait your entire life (ie: "I am a millionaire" vs. "I make a million dollars a year.") Use words like "I am" and "I have", present tense, not "I will be" or "I will have."

Choose to shoot for more than you think you want. Don't say, "I can pay my bills each month." Instead say, "I have abundant wealth and financial freedom." That will make sure that you cover all the bases and don't get stuck with barely enough to get by paycheck to paycheck.

If you are struggling to feel like a good mother, say things like "I am a good mother." "I have gifts and abilities that my children need in order to learn and grow." "I am getting better at being patient and kind to my children." "I am learning to stay calm amidst the chaos of motherhood."

Make sure to recite, read and repeat these affirmations all the time. Over time they will begin to become second nature to you. You will no longer feel cheesy and ridiculous. You will feel empowered and excited.

Here are some powerful affirmations you can copy off of me:

- "I desire to feel like I am worth it."
- "I am learning to love myself."

- "I appreciate my body."
- "I can do hard things."
- "I am a good mother and what my kids need."
- "I enjoy my life and myself."
- "I am my own best friend."
- "I am positive, happy, and full of joy."
- "I love my life."
- "I am choosing to do what is best for me and my family."
- "I have time to learn the lessons I need to become better."
- "I am fun and lovable."
- "I have talents this world needs."

Use these or write your own but start right now. Get a pen and paper and think of the things you want to believe about yourself and your life and go for it. Make sure to put them up in a place you will see them all the time. You can keep it at home or take it to the office. It would be quite a conversation piece with your coworkers if they saw your list, and even more if they heard you say it out loud!

Remember it is okay to feel silly, to be ridiculous, and to laugh at yourself. Make it fun and keep doing it and saying it until you believe it. You will be grateful if you do. I like writing each affirmation on a Post-It-note and placing them all over all the mirrors in my house. This way I am constantly seeing them and even if I am not reciting them out loud, the simple act of reading them reminds me of my desires.

The nice thing about saying these affirmations is that they take very little of your time. You can repeat them while you are putting on your makeup or combing your hair, while you are driving to work, or working out, while you are walking outside or taking a shower.

You can say them in less than a minute! Again, that is $1/1000^{th}$ of your day, so there are no excuses for not doing it. Another thing that takes almost no time, but makes a huge difference in your life, is starting and ending your day with positive vibes.

Set Your Day up for Success

Before I get out of bed in the morning I like to create an image and idea of the perfect day in my mind. I find that when we proactively plan for good things to happen to us, they will.

When my alarm goes off in the morning, I like to start my day by saying things like, "Today is a perfect day." "I make a difference in the world. I am the only one in the world who can do what I do in exactly the way I do it." "I am financially free." "I am happy and living an abundant life in all ways." "I am more than enough and deserve to feel happy." "I am peaceful and have perfect health." You will recognize these as more positive affirmations.

When we think, "Good things are coming my way," they will. Try it! Wake up in the morning and think, "Today is going to be a great day," and it will be.

The opposite is also true. When we start our day with thoughts about how hard it will be and how much we are dreading it, we will experience what it is like to self-sabotage. It is a self-fulfilling prophecy. It is a phenomenon of the universe. We are truly like magnets. What we feel we attract more of (I will cover this more in the last chapter).

Pay attention to your thoughts. Go to bed thinking that you'll wake up feeling refreshed and happy about the events of tomorrow, and you will. Go to bed dreading what tomorrow will bring, and you will have a terrible, no good, very bad day. It happens almost without fail. Once you start to pay attention you will notice it more and more. You should do this in the morning and then again at night. This takes minutes of your time, but yields massive results.

Set yourself up for success for tomorrow by ending your day with positive affirmations about your sleep and what tomorrow will bring. I have found that our bodies will do and feel exactly what we tell them to. It has been fascinating to me that on the days that I go to bed later and still have to get up early, if I tell myself that it will be okay and that I'll wake up feeling refreshed as if I'd had the same amount of sleep as always, I will. If I go to bed worried that I will not get enough sleep and will feel tired the next day, I do. It is amazing.

I usually tell myself that I will wake up before my alarm clock goes off so as to not wake my husband (I get up really early), and almost every time I do, I wake up just before it. I love it. It has revolutionized my life and given me more control over my sleep habits. I know that I am in control of how refreshed I feel, whether I get five hours of sleep or ten, I can feel the same energy if I tell myself I can. You'll learn in the next chapter that getting enough sleep is really important. Ending and starting your day with positive emotions and thoughts will continue the set up for a wonderful day and life.

This brings us to our next life-changing, earth-shattering habit: getting a good night's sleep.

Chapter Highlights:

- "Mirror Work" can have a profound effect on your life. While looking in the mirror you should tell yourself positive things and learn to love and accept yourself.
- It is amazing how quickly the unfamiliar becomes familiar and acceptable with constant repetition.
- Marisa Peer has said, "The easiest and fastest way to gain self-esteem is self-praise." She also says, "The root cause behind every issue is an issue of self-confidence or self-love."
- In today's medical practices we are often addressing the symptoms of an issue without addressing the root cause. While that might take away our pain in the short-term, the pain and disease will always return until we address its source.
- We are all intrinsically enough all of the time.
- Even the most beat-up, weathered and abused bills are still worth the full amount of their value.
- Learning that you are enough all of the time is crucial to your overall happiness. You don't need to prove your value to anyone but yourself.
- To affirm something means to "state or assert positively or maintain as true." When we are feeling low, we can talk ourselves out of that feeling and choose to focus on something that we really want to feel.
- When we say things over and over each day, with *feeling* while we look in the mirror, we start to change our own minds and begin believing them.
- Doing affirmations is another way to re-write the vocabulary used by our inner critics.

- I truly had believed for so long that if I got back to my pre-pregnancy size, I would finally be happy and confident in my body. That was not the case. Happiness is not found in a pants size.
- When writing an affirmation, start with believable phrases that will stretch you a little in the right direction, then add to them as you go.
- The first thing to do is decide what you want. Once you decide what you desire more than anything else (love, riches, health, happiness, etc.) or a combination of them all, you can start writing **positive** affirmations about them.
- Affirmations take very little of your time. You can repeat them while you are putting on your makeup or combing your hair, while you are driving to work, or working out, while you are walking outside or taking a shower. You can say them in less than a minute!
- Before you get out of bed in the morning start to create an image and idea of your perfect day. When we proactively plan for good things to happen to us, we will have success.
- Set yourself up for success for tomorrow by ending your day with positive affirmations about your sleep and what tomorrow will bring.

Actions to Take:

1. Say the words, "I love you and accept you exactly the way you are" while looking in the mirror. Record your initial thoughts and feelings.

   _____

   _____

   _____

   _____

2. Start repeating, "I love myself or I like myself" in front of the mirror, or while you go about your day, as many times as it takes.

3. Think of the things you want to believe about yourself and your life and write several affirmations about them. Keep it positive, short, and believable (baby steps to a complete change of beliefs).

   _____

   _____

   _____

   _____

4. Think of exactly how you want your day to go both before you go to bed and before you get up in the morning. Set your day up for success by starting and ending it the right way!

5. Place your hand on your heart and repeat, "I am a great mom."

HABIT SEVEN:
GET ENOUGH QUALITY SLEEP

"The best bridge between despair and
hope is a good night's sleep."
—E. Joseph Cossman

"Without enough sleep, we all become tall
two-year-olds."
—JoJo Jensen

Do You Get Enough ZZZs?

One of the most important ways to improve our lives is to sleep. Many people are walking around sleep deprived and unable to perform at the top of their game as a result. Sleeping feels good. It makes our bodies function so much better. It is akin to recharging our phone when its battery is low.

I know as a mom with young ones it is incredibly hard to find the time to get adequate sleep. Thinking back on the many sleepless nights and days I had while raising my young children makes me tired. I am not really excited to start the process with this new baby, but I know now that it won't last forever and that I have some powerful things to help me have better sleep.

Nothing can prepare you for being awakened around the clock and having to deal with another person's sleep schedule. It is exhausting. When we feel exhausted, our bodies and minds cannot function like they should. It is imperative to our survival to get proper rest. If you can't sleep, fake it 'til you make it. I heard someone say that if you maintain the sleeping position, even if your mind is wide awake, it is at least giving your body a break. I'm not sure if that is true, but I have tried it on restless nights and have still been able to function the next day, although maybe not as well, so the idea has merit.

I like to leave a paper and pen by my bedside in case my mind is whirling with the things I need to remember to do. When I can't sleep, I write the things down and soon my mind is empty again and I find it much easier to fall asleep. I have to admit however, that I am still not an expert at quieting my mind all of the time when I want to sleep. Lately it seems I get so excited about a project (like this book) that my mind won't let it go and it keeps me up much longer than I planned. This is when I use the trick I talked about earlier – telling my mind that I will be okay no matter how much sleep I get and I believe it. I have always survived, so I guess those results are good enough for me.

The old practice of counting sheep to fall asleep has always bored me. If instead, you practice counting your blessings or thinking of your amazing future, you'll be getting a two-for-one: reprogramming your subconscious mind while getting some zzz's. It's totally better than counting sheep or stars or worrying about what you have to do or have done in the past.

Dear Sleep,

I'm sorry that I hated you when I was a little kid. Right now, I love you very much and cherish every moment with you.

Why is it called "beauty sleep" when you end up looking like a troll?

Take Naps When You Can

Another way to recharge is to take naps during the day. Even a twenty-minute power nap can do wonders for an exhausted body. As a young mother, I was super strict about nap time. I have made it a priority in my life since I was a college student – seriously, I would come home in between classes and sleep. Some of my roommates made fun of me, but it didn't matter. I needed rest and took it when I could get it.

As a mom of younger kids, I made my kids quiet boxes to play with if they weren't napping, and I would sleep while they played. Or I would make it their movie time for the day, so I could rest while they were entertained. It is different for every kid, and some moms don't need naps, but I found it to be my only chance at survival! My kids knew that when it came to nap time, I didn't mess around. They were expected to be in their rooms, or where I had appointed them to be, and they were okay with that. (Except for that nasty phase in which my two young ones didn't like being locked in their room for their own safety.) I think kids secretly crave that time alone as well. It helps them unwind and use their imaginations.

If you don't feel comfortable sleeping while your kids are awake, try to find a friend to swap babysitting/playtime with you. They can be a great lifeline at this time in your life. You can give each other the needed break or time to get things done or rest, while you take turns watching each other's kids. I used to swap 20-30 minutes with a friend for each of us to run or walk around the neighborhood and it did wonders for me. I have found that exercising helps me to sleep a lot better.

Dad: Did you hear about the kidnapping at school?
Kid: No, what happened?
Dad: The teacher woke him up.
—Joke found on Google

What is Your Sleep Number?

Another thing about sleep is that we all need different amounts of it. What works perfectly for one person might be a nightmare for another. According to the National Sleep Foundation "on average, women need twenty minutes more sleep than men"[51]. Some women need more sleep than others and some can't sleep at night if they take a nap during the day. The important thing is to figure out your own sleep needs and satisfy them.

For years I felt groggy and tired when I woke up. I never felt like I had a good night's sleep, and I always felt like I wanted to go right back to bed. Often my muscles ached, and my back and jaw were sore from whatever I was dreaming about. When I learned about the power of the mind and started trying to become a better person, I knew that my problems with sleep would solve a lot of other issues in my life. I started experimenting with sleep and it has had wonderful benefits in my life.

I found that even 15 minutes can make or break how I feel. After weeks of experimenting with how long I needed to sleep, I determined that my body needs right around 7 hours and 15 minutes of sleep a night, with a 20-45-minute power nap in the afternoon. Any more sleep than that and I am a groggy monster. Any less sleep than that and I am a wicked witch. It is incredible the power enough sleep has on our body. I encourage you to experiment with your own sleep schedule until you find your power number.

I have never had a sleep number bed, but I know that a lot of people benefit from them. Finding the best time, place, and quantity of sleep you need can make all the difference to the amount of joy and happiness you feel. It will help you be more present and not wishing you were always in bed.

The Facts About Sleep

Getting sleep not only feels good but is important for our body weight.

Some of you might benefit from learning that when you are sleep deprived, you gain weight, or at the very least hold on to all the weight you have. It is a sad but true reality of our bodies. When our bodies don't get sufficient rest, it doesn't matter how much we starve ourselves, we will not lose much if any weight. Our bodies hold on to every calorie, knowing they will need it to maintain our lifestyle. Calories, by definition, are units of energy. Our bodies know that and hold on to all the energy they can to get us through whatever rigorous schedule we put them through. If they know that they aren't going to get the rest needed, they will hold onto every ounce of energy they can to help us survive. So, if you think you want to lose weight to like yourself more, you might want to start with sleeping better. It is so much easier than dieting or starving yourself.

It is hard to feel joy when you are tired. It is challenging to feel anything but tired when you are tired. You can't be your best when you haven't had enough sleep. There are many negative side effects to not getting enough quality sleep:

- Memory issues
- Trouble with thinking and concentration
- Accidents
- Mood changes
- Weakened immunity
- High blood pressure
- Risk for diabetes
- Weight gain
- Low sex drive
- Risk of heart disease
- Poor balance

Between 50-70 million adults in the U.S. have a sleep disorder. Thirty-seven percent of 20 to 39-year-olds report short sleep duration, while 40 percent of 40 to 59-year-olds report the same.[52] [53]

Since the lack of sleep has so many negative side effects, it would be a great idea to learn how to get a better night's sleep.

How to Lull Yourself to Sleep

There are several things that you can do before you go to sleep to ensure a good night's rest. According to the American Sleep Association, in order to get the best night's sleep possible, we should exercise daily, take a hot shower before bed, avoid bright lights before bed, go outside and get natural sunlight daily, go to sleep as early as possible (preferably before 10 p.m.), get fresh air in your bedroom if possible, and take a short day time nap (no longer than an hour).

Other things that you can do include: avoiding fluids, making it as quiet as possible in the bedroom, sleeping with an eye mask or black-out curtains to make the room as dark as possible, giving your head and feet muscles a massage to relax before sleeping, and replacing TV or screen time with reading something spiritual or uplifting. We should also take advantage of the new blue light options on our devices if we can't go without using them.[54]

In order to get rid of a bad habit, you need to replace it with a good one. One of the biggest time wasters of our day is screen time. Too many of us are addicted to our devices and screens. Trust me, I was as addicted as anyone. There was a time when I couldn't even go a few minutes without checking the latest notification, email, text, pin, ping, etc.

According to a recent 2017 study, the average American adult spends a good sixteen hours a week scrolling their smartphones or apps on their devices.[55] That is the equivalent of almost two and a half hours a day.

In addition, Americans on average still watch more than "7 hours and 50 minutes per household per day" of TV.[56] Imagine what would happen if we replaced a small percentage of our current screen time with "me" time or family time. We would see a drastically happier, more confident and fulfilled society. Rather than wasting hours at a time watching someone else's dreams come true, we would actually be making our own dreams come true.

Once I realized how much time I was wasting scrolling and watching mindless or mind-numbing shows, I decided that I was better than that. I was worth more than I was giving myself. I still watch an occasional movie or episode of a favorite show, but I have found that I prefer learning and developing myself the majority of the time. It makes me feel better.

I have replaced looking at my phone, TV, or iPad at night with reading a good book, writing down things I'm grateful for, working on my goals, and listening to voice recordings of my affirmations. I now sleep so much better without worrying whether or not I'm missing something on social media or comparing myself to someone else or their life. I no longer fret about the alarming things going on in the world because frankly, I usually don't even know about them. I go to sleep with peaceful, uplifting thoughts and it has changed my world.

You Can Retrain Your Brain While You Sleep

Several modern scientists, including Dr. Joe Dispenza and Bruce Lipton, say that the subconscious mind is more susceptible to being rewired while we are in the brain state just before sleep.

For this reason, it is crucial to start preparing your mind for permanent positive change well before going to sleep. What you think about and listen to right before you sleep makes a huge difference in how well you sleep and what you are feeling when you wake up. By simply preparing for and believing in a good night's sleep, you will get one. You can wake up feeling pumped and amazing. I have personally replaced screen time with listening time.

I have made several voice recordings of all the things that I want to accomplish and believe about myself and listen to them every night until I am asleep. It is not unusual to wake up in the middle of the night with my earbuds still in and my phone still on the bed. There are a lot of recordings on YouTube that you could use if you don't want to hear your own voice. There are also a variety of sleep meditations and hypnoses designed to reprogram your subconscious mind for anything you want (love, health, wealth, deep sleep, etc.).

To enhance my voice recordings and my meditations, I play some solfeggio frequencies from YouTube on my iPad or laptop, while recording my affirmations into my phone app. Solfeggio frequencies are very healing and there are many different kinds that offer direct vibrations for the kind of healing or improvement you might want. They have become an indispensable way to lull me to sleep at night, during naps, and on those days when I need to relax.

Side note: I have even asked my massage therapist to start using the healing solfeggio frequencies during my massages, as they seem to relax me even more than piano music! Before you judge me as the spoiled mom getting regular massages, remember this book is all about teaching you to take time and invest in yourself. Getting a massage makes a huge difference in my overall well-being. I couldn't afford them for most of my life, but now that I can, I invest in making myself feel as good as possible. I wish I could help every mom get a regular massage if they wanted it. It definitely helps me sleep better.

Okay, let's get back to the point. Listening to the subliminal messages we want in our lives will improve our lives by reprogramming our subconscious minds without us even knowing. This takes no time away from our usual routine, as we all need to sleep anyway. Replacing screen time or whatever we are doing for our night time routine with this practice, will absolutely revitalize you and help you with whatever blocks you have to your current happiness and success. Isn't it great that we can benefit from sleep in so many different ways? My bedtime routine has made my dreams even more vivid and interesting as well.

That brings us to the next chapter, in which you will learn about making your dreams your reality.

Chapter Highlights:

- One of the most important ways to improve our lives is to sleep. Many people are walking around sleep deprived and unable to perform at the top of their game as a result.

- Leave a pen and paper next to your bed for those nights that your mind is whirling and you can't sleep. Write down all your thoughts and things to do before going to sleep and you'll sleep better.

- Counting your blessings or dreaming of a fantastic future are much better ways to fall asleep than counting sheep.

- If you need them, naps can be a life saver for moms! Do whatever it takes to find some peace and quiet in the middle of the day. Give your kids quiet boxes, put on a movie, or swap time with a friend.

- We all need different amounts of sleep. Figure out your sleep number and make a daily habit of getting that amount of sleep so you can perform at your best.

- Getting sleep not only feels good but is important for our body weight.

- A lack of sleep is detrimental to our health in many ways. More than 50 million adults in the U.S. have some kind of sleep disorder.

- There are many things we can do to assure ourselves the best night's sleep possible.

- In order to get rid of a bad habit you need to replace it with a good one. One of the biggest time wasters of our day in age is screen time.

- You can rewire your brain and learn while you are sleeping.

Actions to Take:

1. Are you getting enough sleep? For the next week, record how many hours of sleep you are getting and how you feel throughout the day. At the end of the week, evaluate and figure out your perfect sleep number, then make a plan to make it happen daily.

2. Find a friend to swap nap time with or come up with a plan to implement daily naps if needed.

3. What ways can you improve your nights' sleep from what was listed in this chapter? Write down at least 3 things you can change tonight if you want to start sleeping better, and do them!

   _____

   _____

   _____

   _____

4. Record your own affirmations and listen to them before going to sleep at night.

5. Place your hand over your heart and repeat, "I am worth a good night's sleep and will do what it takes to be well-rested."

HABIT EIGHT:

FEEL GOOD NOW-
THE POWER OF VISUALIZATION

"If you don't know what you want,
you will probably never get it."
—Oliver Wendell Holmes, Jr.

"You are more productive by doing
fifteen minutes of visualization than from
sixteen hours of hard labor."
—Abraham Hicks

"Visualization is the human beings' vehicle to
the future – good, bad or indifferent.
It's strictly in our control."
—Earl Nightingale

My Wake-up Call

Speaking of dreaming, what do you dream about? I'm not talking about in your sleep, but in your waking moments, what kind of life do you fantasize living? Many people are simply stuck where they are in life because they don't have a vision or a clue about what they really want. They are content with mediocrity and being stuck in the nine-to-five rat-race. If we want to make positive steps that will turn our dreams into reality, we first need to *know what we want* out of life.

We need to train our mind to see and feel and experience what we desire in our future and visualize our dreams.

What do you want?

I know when I first started asking myself this question, I didn't really know what I wanted. I was afraid to dream big. I felt guilty for wanting more money or not appearing content with what I already had. I dreamed of having a happy and healthy family and continuing to live my life the way I was living it. This would have been perfectly fine, had I been truly happy.

After years of sacrificing my time, body, energy and means for my kids and husband, I was burned out and hopeless. I felt like I'd be stuck in a state of mediocrity forever. Then an unexpected tragedy snapped me out of my trance and awakened me to the need to live my life to the fullest.

I was sitting in the dentist's office, waiting for my daughter's teeth to be cleaned, when I got a phone call that would forever change my life. My sister whispered two words that no one ever wants to hear: "Dad's gone." To say this was unexpected and unwanted would be an understatement. I lost it right then and there in the office, in front of the receptionist. I probably cried enough tears to fill their fish tank. My world would never be the same.

My dad passed away at the young age of sixty-two. They found his body crumpled between his exercise bike and couch, with his foot still in the pedal of the bike. He had been trying so hard to fix his heart (he'd had surgery several months prior), that he overdid it. Sadly, he died alone.

His death really got me thinking. He left this world with all the things money could buy, but a life that was filled with loose ends and conflict. He was in a stressful work environment, had strained relationships with some family members, suffered poor health, and was so overworked and tired that he had very little time for play and joy.

He did not plan on leaving the world that way. I don't think anyone really does. In fact, he was working on selling his businesses so that he could retire and spend his days doing what he loved with the ones he loved. That day never came. *We all somehow believe we will have time "someday." But what if someday never comes?*

One of the most tragic things about his passing is the lack of any writings or proof of his existence. While we have several pictures of him, he didn't keep a journal, and we have very few video recordings to remember him by. He was a fantastic writer and song-writer, but we could find no evidence of this besides a few emails, and our memories. He loved hard-work and serving other people, but unless we wrote those things down, they would be forgotten. It was heart-breaking.

This really made me reflect on my own life. What if I were to pass away today? Would I be okay with the legacy I have left?

I love(d) my dad with all my heart, and I am in no way discounting his contribution to my life or to the world.

He was a great man and taught me so much about life and how to treat other people and fight for what we believe in. I just think that if he could, he would choose to redo the last few days if not years of his life.

None of us are ever really promised tomorrow.

It is weird, but I truly feel like my dad's death brought me back to life. It awakened me to the fact that I might not have tomorrow. I began to feel much more keenly the need to enjoy my life *now* and not wait until I could retire to find joy. Did I want to leave this life full of regret, or did I want to pull myself together and live a life I dreamed of? What did I want people to say about me at my funeral?

I did some serious reflection upon my life. Somehow, the bright-eyed, dream-filled girl of my youth was resurrected within me. I was determined to make the most of the one and only life I was guaranteed and to live it to the fullest. But first, I needed to figure out what exactly that looked like. I started dreaming big for the first time in a very long time. It was very liberating.

One day the power in our house went out, and we were unable to flush our toilets. I told the kids they could go to the bathroom outside (so long as it was far away from the house). My daughter, pleasantly surprised by the experience, yelled out, "Mom, I have PEEDOM!! I can pee anywhere I want too!" Grace age 7

Dream Document

I got out some paper and a pen and started writing. I wrote "My Future is so Bright" and then proceeded to write about six or seven pages filled with *exactly what I wanted my life to be like in every way before I died.* This simple exercise and added motivation from my dad's untimely passing, gave me the push I needed to start living my dream life. I started to really see my impossible dreams as reality. It felt invigorating and liberating. I no longer felt tied down to my duties as a wife and mother. I enabled myself to think bigger than my family and to dream about what really truly made me feel alive and happy.

I want you to do the same thing. When you have a few spare moments, start writing down your dream future in as much detail as possible. What will you look and feel like? Where will you live? What will you be doing with your time? A great way to get you started is to answer the question: If time and money were not an issue, what would I be doing right now? Write until you can't possibly think of anything else to add. Make sure that you write in the present tense, as if all of those amazing things you dream of have already been accomplished or are presently in your life. Once you have that Dream Future Document, read it at least once a day.

This can also be a great thing to do with your spouse or partner. Having a common dream and goal for the future really brings solidity and purpose to a relationship. Think about it. Like most moms, you probably once had a vision of getting married and finding the love of your life. Once you did, you probably had to desire to have children, to get a nice house to raise them in, to have enough money to do fun things as a family, etc. etc.

Somewhere along the line, we lose touch with our own dreams and start living for our kids. We allow them to dream and imagine great things (hopefully), while we all but lose touch with our own desires and goals. This can lead to a marriage feeling more like a business partnership than a romance, and a stalemate in our personal development.

Spending one date night, or even a few minutes, with your spouse or loved one to dream big together can be huge for a marriage, or any relationship. It can be the spark a dull relationship needs to rekindle the flame that brought you together in the first place. When you see where you both want to go with the rest of your lives, it can ignite passion in a stale relationship. You can bring yourselves and your love back to life by finding the common ground and going for your dreams together.

When my husband and I did this, it started a new phase of our marriage. For over a year now, our love has grown and we have become inseparable. We have found things that ignite our souls and make us grow together while pursuing our goals and making our future come to life every day. It has been thrilling to feel like we are in the honeymoon stage all over again. Only this time, it is so much better. Our hormones aren't calling the shots, our conscious awareness and desire to make our dreams come true have taken over. We already have the house, the kids, the career, and many years together under our belt, so we are perfecting it and making it even better every day. It has done wonders for our marriage. We feel like young kids again. We are about to celebrate our sixteenth year of marriage, and it thrills me that we are more in love now than ever.

Writing our future both separately and together allowed us to escape from our mundane reality and to live in our own fantasy world every day. It is fun. When was the last time you truly had fun with your partner, or dared to dream like a child?

How to Be Like a Child Again

Do you remember what you dreamed of being as a child? Do you remember the days that you could dream big and honestly believe that you could do anything and be anyone? Kids have the best imaginations and can have tons of fun with only their mind. We can get ideas by listening to what our children dream about and observing how they spend their time.

As a child, I dreamed I was going to be a world-class singer and actress. I would watch Disney movies and sing and dance around the room and not have a care in the world. In my mind I literally became Aurora, dancing with a prince in my dreams. I became Snow White singing to the birds and having them help me clean the house. I knew that I could be anything and have my dreams come true. I believed with all my heart that I could be a princess and sing my way through life.

I don't remember when those dreams were shattered, but there came a point sometime in my young life that I was made to feel that I couldn't do it and I believed it. I was told I was not a princess and essentially threw my crown to the ground and stopped believing in myself. I started believing that rather than taking the lead in my own life story, I should play the part of the back-up actress, waiting in the wings in case I got a chance to shine. I let other people call the shots on my own stage and as a result, I lost my sense of joy and wonder.

My mind slowly became conditioned to the ways of the world, thinking that I had to be "special" or have "amazing talent" to get where I wanted to be, and I just didn't have it. At some point in almost every child's life "reality" hits and they feel their dreams die within them. They start believing the voices of the world rather than the voice in their heart and they let the world dictate who they should become.

"I'm so excited for my soccer game tomorrow. I'm going to score either 7, 10, 5, or 16 goals! I am, Mom, I really am! I believe! I saw it in my mind" Grace 7 years old.

She went on to score 5 goals the next day. Before that, she had only ever scored one goal.

The Ones That "Make it"

Those rare few that actually manage to keep their dreams alive are the ones who make them happen. They are the world-class athletes, the entrepreneurs making millions, the inventors who know that their vision will make a difference, and the people who don't let the limiting beliefs of the world get them down. They choose to believe their heart rather than their teachers, parents, media, or their peers. Their belief allows them to achieve what others would deem impossible.

I have read story after story about famous people knowing a secret that most of the world does not know. They know how to visualize. They know how to dream/envision so intensely and make their visions so real in their minds that it cannot help but happen.

They are the visionaries like Henry Ford. His vision was to make a car that everyone could afford and drive. He didn't let all the naysayers and unbelievers get him down. The company he founded remains to this day one of the leaders in the automobile industry.

They are the actors, like Jim Carrey, who at a time when he was completely broke, wrote himself a check for $10,000,000 for "acting services rendered". Five years after writing that check he received a check for $10 million dollars for his part in the movie, *Dumb and Dumber*.

They are the dreamers like Steve Jobs, who have an idea that they know can revolutionize the world. He built a company like *Apple* in his garage with no money and a few friends that now dominates the field of electronics and is loved in homes around the world.

They are the doctors that can look past the way it has been done and see in their mind a new way to make a surgery work and heal countless lives, like Ben Carson.

They are the poverty stricken, beaten, and sexually abused, like Oprah, who know that they will make it big *no matter what*, and have touched the lives of people all over the planet.

They are the inventors, like Thomas Edison, who failed more than 1000 times before the light bulb actually worked but would not let his dream die. There are dozens or more examples of these leaders who knew how to make what they visualized in their minds happen, regardless of what the world said was impossible, and in spite of what others would consider "failures."

Almost everyone that has made it big has done so by following an unrelenting dream in their minds- a vision of what they could do or become or have- a vision so beautiful it was motivating enough to get back up from all the failures and rejections and keep going until it became reality.

These people inspire me and make me want to live out my dreams!

What all of these incredible people have in common is their ability to see their dreams come true in their minds and to feel as if they are already *living it before it happens*. Bob Proctor, a world-renowned millionaire, author and speaker, likes to say, "When we can see something in our minds, we can hold it in our hands." [57]

Upon learning about visualization, I started feeling like a kid again- I was given permission to dream big and to feel the grandeur of living those dreams in reality. It was as if a switch went off inside my head telling me it was okay to think of the wildest dreams I could conjure up and to feel the immensity of what it would feel like to achieve them. It has been incredible. I have felt on top of the world, even when I haven't experienced the fruits of those dreams yet in my current reality. The more detailed you can make your visualizations, the more real they will become. Although I never felt like a good writer, this book is a result of my big vision of helping millions of people gain self-confidence and joy.

What do *You* Want?

Visualizing is really fun to do. I want you to try something. Sit quietly in a place where you can think and be alone for a few minutes. Now think about something specific that you really want. Get a good image in your mind of that object or thing and take it in. Try to see what it looks like to have it, what it feels like to touch it, what it smells like, tastes like, sounds like, etc. Imagine in the most precise detail you can, feeling as if you already have it and what emotions it allows you to have. Feel those emotions as intensely as you can for as long as you can. When you have come to the point of really experiencing that thing coming to life, take out a piece of paper and write down what it feels like. Include the details you envisioned. This exercise helps us learn how to dream and see things like a child again.

If you didn't already do the "Dream Future Document" I mentioned earlier, this would be a good way to get you started.

One of the key things to note when visualizing or trying to create a new reality in your life is the *feeling* it will bring into your life and why. When we can create the *feeling* of what we want before we have achieved it, it will bring us onto the same vibrational frequency of that thing and will therefore attract it into our lives. It literally releases the same chemicals in our brains that the actual experience would yield and makes us a magnet to them. (more on this in Habit 10).

It is imperative that when we visualize, we get to the point that we *feel* the emotions of having accomplished that dream- we literally experience it to the fullest in our mind, not just see it, but feel it, see it, touch it, and taste it as if we were already there. I learned this from an exercise at a workshop with Dr. Joe Dispenza.[58] He is a leading-edge scientist and author that helps people heal with the power of their mind.

It is a lot easier to get to that emotional level of experience when we know why we want it.

Find Your Why

When you make a goal or dream of your future, do you take the time to figure out the real reason why you want it? If you don't know why, like **really why**, you are setting a goal you are a lot less likely to achieve it. I'm not talking about the superficial why's either, but the deep penetrating, move-you-to-action kind of why. If you want to figure out the why behind your desires, all you have to do is keep asking the question, "why" until you get to the point where you know and feel and experience emotion about it.

If you want to lose weight is it because you think you'll look better? Why? Is it so, you can fit into your clothes? Attract the love of your life? Get compliments from other people? Why? So, you can feel good about yourself?

Every goal we make can be narrowed down to **a feeling** that we long to have.

I promise that if you keep asking, "Why," you will be able to dig deeper and deeper. You need to keep asking yourself why you want something until you come down to that feeling that you want to feel. Every desire we have and decision we make is because of a feeling we think we will get when we achieve it.

Sometimes we have to do things in reverse order in our minds to see the reasons behind doing them. Think about getting into those size __ jeans without having to suck in or jump from side to side. How does it **feel**?

If you want to have more money, why do you want it? So you can pay your bills and be comfortable? Probably not. You more likely want the feeling that comes with financial security. You want to **feel** free from struggles and from worrying and to be able to buy and go where-ever you want, and money allows you to do that!

Do you want a life partner? Do you long for real love in your life? Why? Is it because you want someone to go out to eat with, share experiences with? Yes, but much more important than that, it is because you want to **feel** something, perhaps love?

Maybe it is your desire to learn how to be a better mother or to stop yelling at your kids. Why? Could it be so that you can finally feel good enough, or like you are doing something right? Maybe it is so you can no longer feel guilt or shame, or like you are failing?

We all long to **feel** things deeply in life. When you make any goal, if you truly get down to the heart of the reason why, it is always because of the feeling you want when you achieve it. We all want to feel happy in our own skin, we all want to feel free and secure, and we all really want to feel loved and good enough. Those feelings are at the heart of every goal or desire we have, and the sooner we realize that the better off we will be.

What is preventing you from feeling the way you want to feel RIGHT NOW? Think about what might be holding you back and what you are waiting for and decide to feel it now.

When you learn how to see and feel your dreams in your mind, long before you achieve them, you will enjoy life so much faster and more fully. Can you see the logic in finding the way that those things would **feel** and feeling them first? It makes a lot of sense when you think about it.

So many of us are conditioned to think that once we achieve some goal *then* we will feel happy. Once we get that job, lose that weight, kiss that person, go to that place, *then* we will be happy.

However, if we can learn to be happy first, then the goal is bound to be achieved, because we will be on the same vibrational frequency as that achievement or feeling. Our happiness in feeling what it will feel like before achieving it will propel us forward in the direction of making it happen a lot faster than feeling the lack of not having it. I know that this sounds completely backwards from the way we are normally taught, but once you start practicing it, you will come to learn that we have been taught wrong. It is time to start a new way of thinking and seeing the world. If you don't believe me, keep on doing it the way you've been doing it and keep getting the same results. That is the definition of insanity - doing the same thing over and over and expecting different results.

I now dedicate ten to thirty minutes a day to seeing my dreams come true in my mind. It is part of my morning routine. Once I get into the "zone" after deep breathing, I allow my subconscious to experience my big dreams by visualizing them down to the smallest of details. I try to get to the point where I absolutely feel the most amazing joy from the experience and I often get to the point of shedding tears because thinking of these dreams and seeing them as if they were real is so intense and satisfying. I then thank the Lord for helping me realize those dreams and goals.

What about you? Do you like to see things in your mind and use your imagination? If you haven't done so for a while, now would be a great time to start. Do it with your kids or by yourself, but just do it. Allowing yourself to see things like a child and to believe in your dreams, while knowing why you want them, will bring them into your life.

Now that you have your real *why* in place, we can move on to the next life-hack: goal setting.

Chapter Highlights:

- Many people are simply stuck where they are in life because they don't have a vision or a clue about what they really want.
- Thinking of living as if we were dying can be truly liberating.
- Taking the time and energy to really figure out what we want most of our life and then visualizing it happening can revolutionize our lives.

- We can bring ourselves and our love back to life by finding the common ground and going for our dreams together.
- Kids have the best imaginations and can have tons of fun with only their mind. We can get ideas by listening to our children and hearing what they want and do with their time.
- Those rare few that actually manage to keep their dreams alive are the ones who make them happen. They are the world-class athletes, the entrepreneurs making millions, the inventors that know that their vision will make a difference, and the people who don't let the limiting beliefs of the world get them down.
- Almost everyone who has made it big has done so by following an unrelenting dream in their minds- a vision of what they could do or become or have- a vision so beautiful it was motivating enough to get back up from all the failures and rejections and keep going until it became reality.
- One of the key things to note when visualizing or trying to create a new reality in your life is the feeling it will bring into your life and why.
- When you make a goal or dream of your future, do you take the time to figure out the real reason why you want it? If you don't know why, like **really why**, you are setting a goal you are a lot less likely to achieve.
- Every goal we make can be narrowed down to **a feeling** that we long to have.
- What is preventing you from feeling the way you want to feel RIGHT NOW? Think about what might be holding you back and what you are waiting for and decide to feel it now.

- If we can learn to be happy first, then the goal is bound to be achieved, because we will be on the same vibrational frequency as that achievement or feeling.
- The definition of insanity - doing the same thing over and over and expecting different results.

Actions to Take:

1. What would you do differently today or this year if you knew that you were dying? Write down the dreams and things that you want to accomplish before you die. Ask yourself and answer honestly: If time and money weren't an issue, what would I be doing with myself/my time?

   _____

   _____

   _____

   _____

2. Take some time to really reflect on what you want your future to be like. Write down your "Dream Future Document" (or better yet type it out so that you can tweak it regularly). Write it in the present tense, as if all your dreams have already happened, and try to capture the emotion of it. (If you're like me, you won't even come close to being able to fit it here!) When you are done, make it a daily habit to read and review it.

   _____

   _____

   _____

   _____

3. Take some time to do the same activity with your spouse or partner. Dream big together and awaken the spark in your marriage!

4. Sit quietly in a place where you can think and be alone for a few minutes. Now think about something specific that you really want. Get a good image in your mind of that object or thing and take it in. Try to see what it looks like to have it, what it feels like to touch it, what it smells like, tastes like, sounds like, etc. Imagine in the most precise detail you can, feeling as if you already have it and what emotions it allows you to have.

5. How can you implement a daily practice of visualizing your future into your life?

_____

_____

6. Place your hand over your heart and repeat out loud, "I have the power within to see and create my future. I give myself permission to dream big."

HABIT NINE:

SET GOALS THAT SCARE YOU & SHARE YOUR MASTERPIECE

"Even if you go for it and it doesn't work out, you still win. You still had the guts enough to head straight into something that frightened you. That type of bravery will take you places."
—The Better Man Project

"If you don't design your own life plan, chances are you'll fall into someone else's plan. And guess what they have planned for you?
Not much."
—Jim Rohn

A goal properly set is halfway reached."
—Zig Ziglar

Set Goals

According to *forbes.com* only 3% of adults actually write down their goals and 83% of the U.S. population does not have goals.[59] That means that there are a lot of people out there who are not living a very exciting or passionate life. David Schwartz, in the book *The Magic of Thinking Big*, states, "No medicine in the world—and your physician will bear this out—is as powerful in bringing about long life as is the desire to do something."[60] Goals bring a level of excitement and anticipation in life that we cannot find by other means.[61]

Having goals gives our lives meaning and purpose. It allows us to have a direction and reason for being. Goals help us make progress, which is a key contributor to feeling good about ourselves. Having a sense of purpose and meaning in life enhances our self-esteem, decreases our chances of depression, increases our well-being, and improves our mental and physical health.

Many people are living a satisfactory life. However, if we were to ask every person we meet, "Are you living your life's purpose?" or "Are you satisfied with where your life is headed? How many would answer in the affirmative? Too many of us don't feel like we have a purpose.

Let me guarantee you right now, your life most definitely has a purpose, and finding out what it is will allow you freedom and drive that you have never experienced before. A good way to find out what your personal mission or purpose is here on Earth is to start making and actually achieving some goals.

As a busy mother it can seem impossible to grow in any other way than the direction our children force us to but let me assure you that it is possible. When your dream is sufficiently big and thrilling, you will find the time and means necessary to make it happen. I know several women who are making a full-time income from home with little babies and kids. I also know women that are struggling with chronic diseases, depression, or working full-time jobs outside of the home and still manage to bring their dreams to pass. Anything is possible if we believe it is and have the right *why* and enough drive to do it.

Right now, I am experiencing the most acid reflux I've ever had in my life and yet my goal is to finish this book, so I'm not letting it stop me. I've been typing through the pain and not allowing it to stand in my way. I care more about helping other people than wallowing in my own pain or discomfort. Nothing can stand in the way of a truly determined and passionate desire.

Goal setting has always been a part of my life and it has brought me a sense of direction and clarity. I have learned and adopted a method for goal setting that I have found to really work.

I believe in setting big goals, goals that scare me and seem impossible. If your goals don't scare you, they are not big enough. **Goals scare you when you have no idea how to achieve them.** Setting huge goals sends feelings to your brain that make you realize that you have to change and grow in order to reach them. This can be the catalyst you need to actually get off the couch and do something. When we set little goals that are easily obtainable, or that we already know how to achieve, we often don't feel as motivated to achieve them because we think they are too easy and not worth the effort. We don't get as excited about them, and therefore, do not do them.

It can feel overwhelming after setting a big goal if we set the sights too high and don't know how to get there. If we keep that goal so big that it seems unattainable, we might start off strong, then end up right where we started, then quit. We see this happen every year around the New Year. People set a "New Year's Resolution" and then go full steam ahead, only to peter out about three weeks later, when they find that spending an hour at the gym five days a week is too much for their schedule. Statistics show that only 8% of people who set a resolution on January 1, actually achieve it. That is a pretty significant failure rate. [62]

Don't Give up Before You Even Start

Napoleon Hill, author of *Think and Grow Rich*, once asked an audience, "What is the average number of times that a person tries to achieve a new goal before they give up?" After several guesses from the audience, he gave the answer: "Less than one." His point was that most people give up before they even try." [63]

What things have you wanted to pursue in your life, but were too afraid to try? What goals have you been pushing back or saying, "someday" about? What have you already tried, but given up when the going got tough?

The key to not giving up and failing at our big goals is to keep our *"why"* at the forefront of our minds, and use it as the motivation to keep going when we feel like quitting.

With a compelling *why*, we can then work our way backwards from the big goal until we get to the point where we know what kind of action to take. You can do this by taking that big massive unattainable goal and breaking it down into medium sized goals, then breaking those medium sized goals down until they are so small that you can actually do them right now. Figure these goals out by asking yourself what steps you'd have to achieve to get to the big goal. Make sure you write it all down and come up with a plan of action that seems doable. Remember that "Rome wasn't built in a day". Many of our big dreams and aspirations will take time, patience, several failures, and perseverance to achieve.

One book that I love is called *The Compound Effect*, by Darren Hardy. Although it is a book about finances, it taught me a lot about habits and how doing the little things over and over can yield big results. When we invest a little money in the stock market it can multiply and yield us much more than we invested over time. We too can see the benefits of little efforts compounding to make our lives better. Too often we set huge, unrealistic goals and then quit after a few weeks because we are overwhelmed and feel like we will never achieve them. By breaking down our big goals and taking incremental steps to achieve them, we will begin to see the mountain we've been moving a pebble at a time.

Rather than feeling like we have taken on more than we can chew, we will begin to see that this massive goal doesn't seem so impossible anymore. We begin to believe that we can not only "Dream the Impossible Dream", but we can **achieve it**. For example, I set a goal to be able to do 22 pushups from my feet, not my knees. That may not seem like a huge scary goal to you, but at the time I made the goal, I had never in my life been able to do even one real pushup, and certainly didn't believe I could. It scared me to death!

Today Royal (3-years-old) and I walked to the store to buy Susie a birthday present. As he picked up a toy in excitement, I informed him that while it wasn't his birthday, he might ask Santa to bring him that toy. For the next half hour, he examined almost every toy in several aisles and said over and over, "I want Santa bring me this one!" Of some toys he said he wanted Santa to bring him two. In between toys, he muttered to himself, "Me so excited." Then we left the store and walked by a big truck cab. "I want Santa bring me that one!" he exclaimed. #dreambig (story shared by my cousin-in-law)

Pushups Challenge

It all started after seeing several Facebook posts of people completing a twenty-two-day pushup challenge. People were trying to gain awareness of the unfortunate fact that every day twenty-two war veterans commit suicide. In order to do this, they took video of themselves doing twenty-two pushups every day for twenty-two days. I watched in awe as one of my friends was able to do some crazy pushups- even while doing a wall hand stand. I thought to myself, "Wow, I have never been able to do a 'real' pushup in my life, let alone the fancy kind!"

I remember distinctly those days in elementary school when the physical education teacher would evaluate our fitness level by making us run laps, do sit-ups, pushups and pullups. I always felt really great running and doing the sit-ups, but when it came time to do pushups or pullups, I could never even come close to doing one. I was embarrassed and ashamed. It gave me a sense of failure and like I wasn't fit. The fact that most of the other girls couldn't do them either made me feel slightly better, as misery loves company, but since then, I've always thought of myself as a wimp. As part of my personal development journey I have tried to transform myself in every way. I figured it was time to prove to myself that I was not a wimp. I wanted to get rid of that label that I put on myself long ago. Up until the day I made the goal to do a pushup, whenever exercise videos would require me to do pushups, I always opted to do them on my knees. Even that was hard for me. I'm not even kidding either. I could do maybe twenty pushups on my knees before collapsing. I tried several times to do one real one, to no avail. I couldn't even get half way down. I felt like I had a bad back and neck and that pushups would make me hurt more. I feared the pain and preconceived failure more than the reward.

I have always had profound respect and admiration for our active military and veterans, and those who have sacrificed their lives for our freedoms. I have a real soft spot for those who come home from war with physical disabilities and mental instabilities. My grandfather was one of them and taught me deep love and appreciation for their service. When I saw these posts to help gain awareness for them, my heart longed to help, but my mind told me that I would fail if anyone asked me to do so. It was one of those challenges people have to choose you for or tag you in, and I prayed that no one would ask!

There was no way at that time that I would have been able to video myself doing even one pushup, and I was really ashamed of that. I had been lifting light weights for about a year doing the Hammer and Chisel and 21-day fix extreme workout videos, but I was proud of myself for getting up to twelve-pound dumbbells at that point. Even with weight-lifting however, I still struggled with pushups. Well, my inability to help someone willing to die for my freedom, sparked in me a desire to be able to do twenty-two full pushups. I was anxious to prove to myself that I could do hard things and I challenged myself to accomplish this goal- without any need or desire to post it anywhere, but just to prove to myself that I could.

Breaking down the big goal, I attempted one pushup every morning until I could do one. It took about 3 weeks before I felt like I really had mastered one pushup, but I did it! At that time, I could go all the way down, touch my nose to the ground and actually come back up. I can't even explain how amazing and proud I felt after accomplishing that first pushup. After that I tried to do two a day. It took me another week, then after a month, I was easily doing five pushups every morning.

It was ridiculous and shocking how out of breath I would sound after doing them, and how long it took me to get my breathing back under control, but I did it. I would go on walks with my son around our pond, and then we would stop every lap and try to do five pushups. I felt so elated being able to do that, and he would laugh at my silliness of doing happy dances after performing such a miraculous feat. For him, five pushups was easy. After about three months of doing five, then seven, then eight pushups, I finally got to where I could do ten full body pushups. It was an *amazing accomplishment*, and I felt so good seeing my progress and knowing that I was almost halfway to my goal. After about another month I hit the fifteen-mark and felt great. However, I got stuck at fifteen for another two months- it was like I had a mental block preventing me from getting any farther.

About that time, I had to deal with two major emotional losses in my life. My father and grandfather passed away within two months of each other. I continued to do my morning stretches, but my heart and mind weren't in them. I still challenged myself to do pushups, but I didn't like it, and found myself slipping a little bit.

When I got home from my grandpa's funeral, I decided I needed to get myself out of my funk and do something good for myself. I had to continue to do things that would improve my emotional well-being. At this point, I had started really getting into studying about our thoughts and how the way we feel attracts either good or bad things to us. I started working on my thoughts and trying to be positive and believe in myself regularly. I found myself thinking about being stuck at fifteen pushups. One night I decided, "tomorrow I will be able to do twenty pushups for grandpa," and I believed it.

The next day when I went to do my pushups it felt like a breeze, and I was able to finish twenty pushups for the first time ever. It was a glorious day. The following day I did twenty-two and dedicated them to my grandpa for his service and his life. I learned that I had been the only one holding myself back. My back and neck had not been holding me back, it was my limiting belief. It was my thoughts. I honestly believed that I could not do a pushup and so that is what I did (or didn't do!). However, once I learned that my mind has control over my body and I can teach it new beliefs that would empower me to grow in ways I never dreamed of, I felt amazing.

Proving to myself that I could do twenty-two pushups ignited in me a desire to do even more. I made a lofty goal of being able to do 100 pushups. I know it sounds crazy, but I put it on my vision board and kept working, taking daily baby steps. One day, I felt particularly great in the morning and decided I was going to do more than twenty-two pushups by the time I went downstairs. I started the morning with thirty pushups. I thought to myself a little while later, "well, I'm already a third of the way to 100. Maybe I should try to do 100 in a day." So, I did ten pushups every time I had to go to the bathroom. By the end of the day I was at 84 pushups and feeling pretty sore. I knew that I was pushing my luck and that I should probably leave the accomplishing of the goal to another day, as this was the first time I had tried. I went to bed having done an incredible 84 full body, nose-to-the floor type pushups, and feeling higher than a kite on a windy day.

Within a week, I was able to do a whopping 103 pushups in a day. I cannot tell you the exhilaration and emancipation I felt from accomplishing this miracle. I was on Cloud Nine, better than I've ever felt, and especially more confident than ever. I learned at that moment that I can accomplish anything I put my mind to. I felt incredible. I now set the goal of doing 100 pushups in 100 minutes, and I know that I'll achieve it someday. I love knowing that I can do hard things if I believe I can. You can too. The sky is the limit!

I feel alive knowing that I could do the challenge for five soldiers, not just one. If I can do it, anyone can. Believe me when I say I was a wimp among wimps. For years I believed I couldn't do it, and therefore I couldn't. When you change your mind about what you are capable of, there is no stopping you. Now that I've "mastered" the pushup, I think I'll give pullups a try. That is the thing with goals—we need to keep setting them. Never settle for where you are but keep moving onward and upward.

Got 4-Minutes?

Perhaps, for you, doing one or even one hundred push-ups is no big deal. I realize that many people are a lot stronger and more fit than me, and I'm okay with that. I learned through this challenge that exercise (something that I could never find the time for before) was possible on any schedule. If I could benefit from doing ten pushups or squats (or whatever move I wanted) several times throughout the day, then I could fit exercise into my life. I knew that exercise was another component of a happy and healthy life, but until this goal I didn't really make the time for it. I was thrilled when I found out that Harvard researchers verified that working out in pieces throughout the day was as beneficial as doing it all at once, "as long as the energy expended is the same."[64]

Exercise is an important thing to try and fit into our lifestyle. It makes us feel good, increases our energy, improves our health, and helps burn calories so we can eat more of the foods that we might feel are "forbidden." For this reason, I thought some moms could benefit from some of the information I found.

The latest research on exercise and fitness actually says that you can replace one hour in the gym with as little as four minutes of exercise at home. When I heard that, I knew I'd found something totally doable for moms or any busy person for that matter! If getting fit is something you want to learn more about, there are many easy mom-oriented workouts you can find online, even some that involve the kids. I love the idea of a four-minute workout, which you can find on YouTube.

The most important thing is to find some kind of movement that you love and will actually do. I love to ride my bike, go for long walks, hike, and roller blade.

I also enjoy workout videos when the weather isn't inviting. Find something that you don't hate and do it as often as you can!

Okay, now back to the real habit I wanted to focus on in this chapter...

Celebrating the Little Things

I like writing to-do lists. They make it easy for me to see everything I need to accomplish in a day or a week. I used to write really long lists that included every little detail and thing I needed to do in the day. However, the more I researched stress, the more I learned that my lists were actually causing me more angst than they were helping me. I have almost done away with them. My old lists were actually long enough that no one could accomplish them in a day, yet I'd beat myself up at the end of the day when I still had things I hadn't accomplished. I didn't account for the many interruptions that made it impossible to accomplish the impossible. I wanted to be "perfect", and instead of finding great satisfaction in crossing off the things I had accomplished, I focused on the things that I still had to do.

On my quest for greater happiness, I have learned that instead of making a list every day, it is much more relaxing and beneficial (for me) to make one for a week. Then, by the end of the week, I can easily accomplish everything on that list and feel good about myself. I still have to calendar events and appointments so as to remember daily details, but my list is no longer a mile long. Instead, I focus on the top 5 things I can do every day from my weekly list. It was like taking a huge weight off my back.

I also learned the power of celebrating the small wins in life. Instead of feeling like a failure because I didn't check everything off my list, I started to write or mentally rehearse a TA-DA list. I started looking at the many things that I had done rather than dwelling on the few things that I hadn't gotten too. I gave myself credit for what I'd accomplished and started celebrating the baby steps, like doing a happy dance after achieving one pushup. Rather than feeling overwhelmed looking ahead at all the steps left, if we look behind occasionally and give ourselves a big hug or a pat on the back for how far we have come, it will feel really good.

Learning how to celebrate the little victories each day brings me greater happiness than fretting over the unaccomplished. When we learn to take the time to have a mini party or dance celebration or woo-hoo moment after achieving something, we are more likely to convince our subconscious mind of the joy of pursuing that goal.

Don't think that the little things don't matter. It may feel like you are covering the miles as slowly as a turtle, but soon you'll arrive at your end goal and realize how many miles you've enjoyed, and you will feel amazing. Don't let the seemingly slow pace of progress become an excuse to quit or give up or get down on yourself. Even if you only spend five minutes a day toward your goal, you will get there faster than if you don't spend any time at all!

Something I came up with to accompany my TA-DA list and make it easier to see the daily pebbles moved, was to make a TA-DA jar. Take a mason jar and label it with "TA-DA" and "PT" on it. I said to label it "PT" for two reasons: 1) it can stand for Positive Thinking. When you catch yourself in the act of being mindful and re-training your brain, celebrate it! 2) Party Time!

You then put a coin in the jar for every little thing you accomplish in the day. This could be getting something on the to-do list done, or just catching yourself in a wrong track in your mind and changing it. Every time you improve or progress, if you put a coin in the jar, it will motivate you to do more.

It's very similar to a sticker chart for children when they are potty-training. There is just something psychologically uplifting about celebrating the little things and seeing your improvements. You choose how big of a coin you deserve for each accomplishment. Some might be worth a penny, some a quarter, and if you really feel amazing, why not put a dollar or two in there. When your jar is full, you can use that money to treat yourself to something really fun and make it a party. Over the course of a few weeks, you will find that seeing the jar fill up will help you want to do more and more things to literally see the mountains move in your life.

Celebrate every mile-marker on your journey and you'll find you love the journey and no longer fear or long for what is up ahead. You are bound to realize your goals and find your purpose and passion in life the more you work toward them and celebrate even the smallest of progress. Your purpose and passion will bring about your personal masterpiece.

My daughter was around four-years-old and had just finished "playing" the piano with the rest of the family in different rooms. After about 10 seconds of silence, she loudly remarked, "I don't hear any clapping or 'good-jobbing!" So, of course, claps began throughout the house, and we all told her how wonderful her playing was. Facebook Friend

---

What Will Your Masterpiece Be?

Finding and sharing your masterpiece with the world will make you feel amazing- it will get you out of the ditch that you didn't know you were in. Many people find that when they live their passion, they naturally attract the money or things they need to survive without having to sacrifice their love of that passion. So many people are living lives they do not love five days a week so that they can enjoy two days a week. It is a sad realization of where we are as a culture. For moms, even the weekends don't seem like a break—they are more of the same. Without a true passion and goal, we can feel like we are losing ourselves and limiting our personal growth.

For many years I thought I was perfectly content and ok with my day job of staying home and making sure the house was clean, the laundry washed and folded, the food cooked, and the bills paid. I did like these jobs most of the time. However, I can't remember one time wanting to get up early so that I could start cleaning toilets or get clothes in the washing machine. These things, while they fulfilled me, did not light me on fire.

In fact, to be perfectly honest, most of the time I found them to be monotonous and boring. I found that I could make them more fun by listening to my favorite music or podcasts and trying to learn and "whistle" while I work. However, when I figured out that I was meant to do something far more than change my kids diapers and make their school lunches, when it dawned on me that I could make an even more far-reaching effect on mankind, not just my own family, I began to see life in a new and much brighter way. I was profoundly changed by the idea that I didn't have to be stuck washing dishes and cooking meals the rest of my life. That was not my main purpose or objective any more. I am truly grateful that there are people out there that love those things (and maybe someday I'll find someone to do them for me!), but I found it wasn't my purpose on this planet. This realization brought new life and meaning to my existence and got me all fired up to become better than I knew how to be.

For the first time in forever (cue Frozen soundtrack), I found myself excited to get up in the morning, not even wanting to sleep for the joy I knew I'd experience in my "day job." I found that during my visualizations I could absolutely make my wildest dreams come true, and make it feel like Christmas morning every morning. The more I felt and believed those visions, the more I was inspired with new ideas as to how to make them my reality.

Magical Mornings

I began getting up early on purpose, even though I'm in the sweet spot of mothering and I have the entire day while my kids are at school to spend how I want. I found that I craved even more time to really get to know myself and connect with my higher source of power. I have learned that getting up early, before any of the little ones are awake, can make or break a mom's day. For me, it was both refreshing and rejuvenating.

I know this sounds counter-intuitive. I talked earlier about getting enough sleep, but I assure you that when you find your sleep number and make it a point to stick to it, you can always find the time to make yourself a priority. For me, that meant going to bed early (9 p.m.) and getting up around 4:30 a.m. Yes, you read that right. It didn't start out that way. I had to wean myself off of too much sleep (that I honestly believed I had to have to survive).

However, after just a few days of practicing getting up before my kids, I was hooked. It was just what I needed to start my day off on the right foot. I found that the more I did it, the more I wanted it. I went from getting up at 6, to 5:30, then eventually to 4:30 in the morning. Don't worry, I don't expect you do to the same thing. I'm just sharing what it has done for me, for those of you who really crave alone time and don't know how to get it. Some of you might prefer doing this kind of thing late at night. Find what works for you.

I found that by the time my kids woke up (around 6:30), I had already stretched, meditated (or deep breathed/practiced mindfulness and visualization), read something uplifting like my scriptures, exercised and showered.

Yes ladies, I am being for real. If I could fit all of the most important parts of self-care into the early morning hours of my day, the rest of the day seemed like a breeze. I was physically, emotionally, spiritually, and energetically prepared to meet whatever came at me. It felt like I had come upon a magical way of dealing with the pressures and stresses of not feeling like I could ever fill my own cup. Although I started this practice a few years ago, I still find myself doing it even while pregnant (although I might sleep in until 5:30 now).

Getting up early gave me the time I needed to rejuvenate my soul and meet the demands of the day. Never once have I regretted getting up. I would much prefer feeling productive, refreshed, and ready to go than dragging myself out of bed because my kids are up. When that used to be the case, I was most often cranky and still tired, making for an awful attitude to start my day off with the kids. Learning to find time for me was crucial. I hope by now you feel like it is crucial for you as well. You have at least 10 minutes a day to refresh and feel vibrant and like you are taking care of you. If you want it bad enough, you will find the time.

I must admit, I don't think I could have done even a portion of what I can do now, when I had small children at home. I was too tired to even attempt magical mornings, or at least that is what I believed.

Having all my kids at home was a great time and I truly loved spending those days teaching and playing with them. However, I am so grateful now to be able to "BE ME" again. For those of you still in the "trenches" of young kids at home all day, don't lose hope. There is light at the end of the tunnel, and inside the tunnel as well. Before you know it, your little ones will be gone all day and you'll be able to find yourself again. Enjoy them while you can and make the most of the precious time you have with them.

For those of you juggling a job away from home and from the kids, these tips can work for you as well. Please don't feel like because you are gone all day you have to spend every left-over moment at home with your kids. The entire family benefits when the mom takes care of herself and has a full cup from which to pour into them.

Using the tools I have taught so far in this book should help moms in every walk of life enjoy the job much more.

I didn't know most of these tips and tricks before my children were all in school. Hopefully, they help you thrive and find yourself thrilled to be alive, even while in the "trenches".

I hope you find true joy in being a mother or homemaker **now**, not when your kids leave the house (or grow out of diapers and car seats). I guess I will get another try at it here pretty soon with another baby. This time I am determined to never feel like a failure, to celebrate the little things and know that I am enough. I am going to know how to love what I am doing and find joy even on the hardest of days.

Only time will tell how I handle magical mornings with a newborn. But, if they don't work out due to the sleepless nights, I am not going to beat myself up about it. I know that this too shall pass, and I need to spend my time cuddling my little one while I can before she grows too big! I'll get back into the habit as soon as I possibly can because I want to keep feeling the best that I can, and my "Magical Mornings" do that for me.

Having all the "must do's" done before the kids get up allows for a lot more free-time and spontaneity during the rest of the day. I now have a lot more time to balance being a mom and work on my goals.

What if You Fail?

Hollywood actor, Jim Carrey, gave a graduation speech at Maharishi University 2014, in which he said that he watched his dad, a natural born comedian, choose a job as an accountant because it was "safe", then get laid off from it 10 years later. He said, "I learned that if you can get fired at a job you hate, you might as well go for the one you love!"[65]

I love that advice.

How many of us are wasting the talents that God has given us? How many of us are more scared of what others will say than how we will feel when we pursue our dreams?

So, what if you fail? If you shoot for the moon, you will probably make it a lot higher than if you shoot for the nearest job available, and you will certainly learn a lot of lessons on the way. Every person on this planet has amazing abilities and talents.

Every one of us has "music inside" or a "song to sing." We were all blessed with different things that we understand, different desires in our hearts and a vast array of creativity and abilities. As mothers, we need to stop comparing ourselves to other mothers or people who appear to "have it all" or that are doing a "better job" than us. Who says so? The God I know and believe in, believes in me enough to have sent me the particular children I have, knowing that I would be the best woman for the job.

Each of us have different talents and abilities, that if used correctly, can bless not only our children, but countless others as well. We would be much better off developing our own gifts than worrying about how they compare to other people's. We are not competing with fellow moms. Instead, we should be encouraging, supporting, and being there for each other. When we collaborate and put our talents together, we can create magic.

Some people are gifted with their hands and can make amazing works of art, buildings, paintings, furniture, etc. Others are gifted with their voices and can give eloquent and motivational speeches, sing arias, coach thousands, or calm others down. Still others are blessed with creativity and ingenuity and can imagine the most incredible things and then make them come to pass. If we do not try, we will never know how far we could go.

What special talents and abilities have you been blessed with? What would you like to develop more or learn? What do you have to offer this world that is uniquely yours? What will pursuing your goals and dreams do for your children?

Carl Jung, a famous Swiss psychiatrist and psychoanalyst who founded Analytical Psychology, said, "Nothing has a stronger influence psychologically on their environment and especially on their children than the unlived life of the parent."[66] Your children are watching and learning from you, mama. When you embrace your superpower(s) and recognize the unique and amazing person that you are, you will not only change the world, you will raise the future generation to do the same!

YOU-nique

When standing on the sand, or even playing with it, the grains all seem to be the same, nothing unique to them at all. However, when you put a tiny pinch of sand under a high-powered magnifying glass, you'd be amazed at the vast array of different colors and textures, sizes and shapes within. Snowflakes are similarly unique and breath-taking upon microscopic inspection. Just like snowflakes and sand, we each offer the world something unique.

Even if someone else has the "same" talent as you, you have a different background and voice. It is good to have a variety of singers singing the same song, or a plethora of restaurants to choose your favorite hamburger to eat. Variety is the spice of life, and *your* spice will add zest to the right people.

You may think that other people are above and beyond what you could ever do. You might feel intimidated and inferior and feel deep down that you will never be as good as someone else. Maybe you feel like you do not have any unique talents or ideas, or if you do have them, you have no idea how to execute them. Perhaps you are so scared of failing or messing up, that you don't even want to try.

Think of it this way, you might never be as good as some of the best, but your voice/talent can and will be heard by those who need it. There will always be others who can relate to your story. The more vulnerable you make yourself today, the more people you will attract to your corner. People love other people who they can understand and relate to. Your particular upbringing, experiences, stories and voice are exactly what someone out there needs to hear. Stop getting in your own way and start thinking about how you can help uplift, inspire, and help others out. Think about what kind of legacy you want to leave. *Once you learn to believe in yourself, others will believe in you too*.

You are the only one who can develop your talents, no one else can do that for you. You alone can lose weight off your body, create your own masterpiece, and tell your own story, so you might as well make it the best story you can write. Live your life so that when you are on your death bed you can say, like Florence Foster Jenkins, "People may say that I couldn't [write, sing, dance, build, create, talk...] but they cannot say I didn't [try]!" What a perfect way of looking at things from the bright side. It's too bad that the majority of people in today's world are holding themselves back and not trying.

In the book *The 10 Pillars of Wealth*, Alex Becker says, "If you look at any city highway at 8:00 a.m., you will see tens of thousands of people with big goals. Goals of fame and fortune, goals of becoming a professional chef or a TV news anchor, goals of making millions and buying houses for everyone they know. All of them are just waiting for the right moment to open their business and live life on their own terms."[67]

Many times, we don't pursue our goals because we are stuck in a job that we hate but don't know how to leave. We live in fear and let it prevent us from leaving our comfort zone. But when we really think about it, how comfortable is that "comfort zone?" I have a friend that refers to it as the "comfy cage." It holds us back from becoming who we were born to be. Leaving it just might be the best thing that ever happens to us, even if it scares us to death.

How long are you going to wait to make your dreams come true? Your dreams are on hold only as long as you hold them back. You can't blame your lack of progress or inability to try on your children. They might be taking up the majority of your time, but when you are truly passionate about achieving something, you will do it no matter what.

Don't Die with Your Music Still in You

Do you have a dream you are too scared to go for?

Ask yourself, what am I really afraid of? What have I got to lose? Will I be proud of myself 10, 20 or 30 years from now if I don't go for it now?

Well, I say, "Go for it! Just do it! If you have a song in your heart, sing it! If you have a book in your mind, write it! If you have a product or business you want to create, then create it! If you have a dream to be a star athlete, famous person, or ANYTHING, go for it! There are people defying the odds every day, why not be one of them?"

Our children will be much more inspired and moti-vated to pursue their dreams if they see us doing the same. I've heard two quotes in the last few months that have changed my life and made me do things that I thought were uncomfortable and hard.

1. *"Many people die with their music still in them. Too often it is because they are always getting*

ready to live. Before they know it, time runs out." Oliver Wendell Holmes Sr.

2. *"The graveyard is the richest place on earth, because it is here that you will find all the hopes and dreams that were never fulfilled, the books that were never written, the songs that were never sung, the inventions that were never shared, the cures that were never discovered, all because someone was too afraid to take that first step, keep with the problem, or determined to carry out their dream."* Les Brown [68]

Are you still getting ready to live? I had to wait until I was 37 years old to be bold enough to "go for it." I'm hoping that this book will inspire much younger women to take a chance on themselves and to believe in their innate power to change the world, or at the very least to change themselves. It really doesn't matter your age. Whatever dream you have in your heart, it is never too late to start going for it. I once heard that Colonel Sanders (the founder of Kentucky Fried Chicken) was in his late 60's and completely broke before his fried chicken made him a legend.

Don't die with your music still in you. You have a voice and a talent that the world needs to hear. Your voice is unique and needed, no one has the same story or talent as you. Stop worrying about what other people think. Stop caring about failing. In my world, there are no such thing as failures, they are just stepping stones to bring you closer to your dream. Don't be afraid to shine your light and let your talents and strengths bless the world. The only time you really fail is when you either don't try or give up trying. Start today and never give up. Your "music" needs to be heard- even if it sounds like you are honking your own horn. I love it when I pull up next to someone in my car and see them belting out to their music and dancing without a care in the world. More of us need to be like that. Instead, so many of us are living with our heads buried in the sand, or worse, like a chicken with their head cut off.

To Fly Means to Truly Live

I recently saw the funniest thing –I was driving home and saw a little bird running as fast as it could in front of my car. I was driving straight towards it, yet it continued to run. I chuckled and was amazed at how fast its little legs could go. I felt like I was watching a live cartoon. I had never really seen a bird run before except for my chickens and they were never that fast. I wondered what this little bird was thinking. It was clearly not injured and could have very easily used its wings to fly to its destination, at a much greater speed than its tiny little legs could carry it. But it seemed to be totally unaware of its ability to fly. It was clueless as to what it was capable of, clearly having no intention of flying, no matter how close my car got to it. This little bird appeared to be acting under the limited belief that it couldn't fly and was only capable of running. It got me laughing and thinking.

Is it possible that the bird heard voices in its tiny little head saying, "You can't fly! Who are you to even try?" Maybe the bird doubted its ability to fly. Perchance it was too busy complaining about the hot pavement to look up and realize it didn't have to deal with it. Or perhaps it saw a bigger bird in the sky and thought there was no way it could ever become that big and graceful, so it shouldn't embarrass itself. It could be that the last time the bird flew it accidentally ran into another bird's nest, and it couldn't live with the guilt and pain inside, so it punished itself from ever flying again. Or maybe it didn't know how to fly? These are all common traps that we mothers get caught in.

How many of us are behaving like this little bird, and living without fully knowing who we are or what we are capable of? How many of us run around thinking only of getting to our destination without enjoying how we got there? How many of us are listening to the voices in our head or around us and allowing them to call the shots in our lives? How many of us are denying ourselves a true glimpse in the mirror to see where we can and should become better and develop our talents and abilities so as to fly? How often do we as mothers feel so frazzled and "busy" doing the same things, that we don't have time for the ones that light our souls on fire and make us feel good?

I recently watched the wonderful movie, _Breathe_[69], based on a true story. It is about a young couple who married and then faced a huge trial. The young woman finds out she's pregnant and when she gets close to giving birth, her young, athletic war-veteran-of-a-husband contracts polio. At that time, polio was a death sentence and caused those who contracted it to live in pain and misery until they passed away. They became quadriplegics, paralyzed from the neck down. Polio victims can't do anything for themselves, are fed through a straw and live off ventilators. For years, these unfortunate people were stuck in hospitals and treated like prisoners, captive to the doctors and nurses who kept them alive.

This young man, Robin Cavendish, begged his wife to get him out. He basically gave an ultimatum saying he wanted to die or get out of that prison. His wife made it possible. She had some nurses and friends literally sneak him out of the hospital when the head doctor wasn't watching and brought him home. They had some hard times adjusting to life with a ventilator, but together created many of the conveniences that are now a part of countless handicapped people's lives.

Robin had the original idea for a wheelchair and a portable ventilator. He was able to travel around and even figured out a way to get onto a plane and fly. Eventually, he came to the conclusion that he had to help all of his fellow "prison mates" escape. He says, "I don't want to just survive, I want to truly live." Instead of falling victim to his circumstance, he used it to create a better life for millions of people.

We all have that same ability within us to set ourselves free from the bondage of our old paradigms or beliefs and to grab hold of a new life. To truly live. To fly. We can take charge of our future by replacing our limiting beliefs with empowering ones. We can feed our inner warrior every day and starve the inner critic. We can meet our own needs and be a good mother at the same time!

Everything around us and in our lives is an external manifestation of an internal belief. If we want to truly live and to have the best kind of life that will be remembered, we need to make that choice today. We must stop giving in to mediocrity and wasting our lives away. We must choose to take advantage of the days, hours, and minutes that we have been blessed with and realize that we can, and should, have something better. We need to make the most of each present moment and stop putting off for tomorrow what we could be doing today. We are the only ones to determine how much joy we will have on our journey and how much love we feel.

If you were diagnosed with a life-threatening disease today, what would you do? What/who would matter most to you? What if you knew that today would be your last day on Earth? Would you be content and feel like you already have and are what you dream of? Or would you feel remorse and regret, wishing you had done more, helped more, traveled more, or become more?

I love the song, *"Live Like You Were Dying"* by Tim McGraw. It has a great message, for we all should live every day as if it's the last and do everything that we love the most. We should do what we dream about and make the most of every minute we have, for we truly never know when it will be our last.

I don't know about you, but I want to fly for as much of my life as I can. I want to teach my children how to fly by doing it myself, not by showing them movies of another person flying. I don't want to wait until I can retire to try, I want to fly now. I want to shake off any fear and doubt that holds me captive and take the leap. Are you with me? Ask yourself, "If not now, then when? If not me, then who?"

This brings us to the last and final habit. When we live a life that we love and truly find our purpose and what drives us, we won't really have a problem with this habit. Until then, I feel like it is one of the most important abilities to develop in our lives. It ranks right up there with being grateful. For that reason, I saved it for last- thus this book begins and ends with the most powerful of habits.

Chapter Highlights:

- I recently learned that only 3% of adults actually write down their goals and 83% of the US population does not have goals.
- Goals bring a level of excitement and anticipation in life that we cannot find by other means. Having goals gives our lives meaning and purpose. It allows us to have a direction and reason for being.
- When your dream is sufficiently big and thrilling, you will find the time and means necessary to make it happen.
- If your goals don't scare you, they are not big enough. Goals scare you when you have no idea how to achieve them.
- Statistics show that only 8% of people who set a resolution on January 1, actually achieve it. That is a pretty significant failure rate.
- The key to not giving up and failing at your big goals is to keep your "why" at the forefront of your mind and use it as the motivation to keep you going when you feel like quitting.
- Learning how to break down the big scary goals into smaller manageable ones will help you achieve them.
- Remember that "Rome wasn't built in a day." Many of our big dreams and aspirations will take time, patience, several failures, and perseverance to achieve.
- The latest research on exercise and fitness actually says that you can replace one hour in the gym with as little as four minutes of exercise at home.

- Instead of making a list every day, it is much more relaxing and beneficial to make one for a week.
- Celebrate your small achievements. Learning how to celebrate the little victories each day brings me greater happiness than fretting over the unaccomplished.
- Finding then doing the things that "light your soul on fire" will bring great happiness to your life.
- Magical mornings saved my sanity, might they do the same for you?
- There is no such thing as failure (unless you don't try, or quit). Use each "failure" as a stepping stone or learning experience on your path to the person you long to become.
- Are you still getting ready to live? I think our children will be much more inspired and motivated to pursue their dreams if they see us doing the same.
- Your children will be much more inspired and motivated to pursue their dreams if they see you doing so first.
- We all have the same ability within us to set ourselves free from the bondage of our old paradigms or beliefs and to grab hold of a new life. To truly live. To fly.
- Everything around us and in our lives is an external manifestation of an internal belief.

Actions to Take:

Answer the following:

1. What things have you wanted to pursue in your life, but were too afraid to try? What goals have you been pushing back or saying, "someday" about? What have you already tried, but given up when the going got tough?

    _____

    _____

    _____

    _____

2. Make a "TA-DA" jar or "Party Time" jar and reward yourself when you make baby steps towards your goal.

3. What talents and gifts have you been given? What have you put on the back burner in order to be a mom? How can you start taking time each day to develop and use your talents? Write down a plan of action to start making your dreams come true.

    _____

    _____

    _____

    _____

4. What big goals do you have that scare you? Simply writing your goals down here and then deciding to take baby steps toward them will give you motivation to progress towards them.

_____

_____

_____

_____

5. Do you know anyone who "died with their music still in them?" How can you prevent that from happening to you? What can you do differently to start "living like you were dying?"

_____

_____

_____

_____

6. Place your hand on your heart and repeat out loud, "I give myself permission to pursue my dreams, knowing that I cannot fail."

HABIT TEN:
DON'T WORRY, BE HAPPY

"Worrying is like a rocking chair, it gives you
something to do, but it gets you nowhere."
—Glenn Turner

"I live by this credo: Have a little laugh at life
and look around you for happiness instead of
sadness. Laughter has always brought me out
of unhappy situations. Even in your darkest
moment, you usually can find something to
laugh about if you try hard enough."
—Red Skelton

"A smile is a curve that sets everything straight."
—Phyllis Diller

Are You a Chronic Worrier?

I don't know about you, but I used to have a terrible addiction to worrying. I thought that worrying about something or imagining the worst-case scenario of a situation meant that I could somehow feel better about it or solve it. If there was an Olympic Competition for worrying, I probably could've won the gold medal. Seriously. It didn't seem to matter what the subject or problem was, I could always find a way to make it worse or think of the worst thing that could happen.

I was like this as a child, but when I became a mother the problem absolutely became my way of life. I was worried if my child would make it through the night. I put each of my kids right next to me during the first 6-8 months of life to make sure they were breathing all night long. But don't worry, I didn't have them next to me on my bed. No, I made a way to keep them in their car seats next to my bed, because I worried that if I had them next to me I'd roll over them or smother them with my blankets. Why the car seat? Because they all had acid reflux and would gag in the middle of the night, and I couldn't sleep with that!

I've worried that my kids wouldn't learn to walk or talk or would be outcasts at school. I worried that they would not find the right friends, have the best teachers, eat the healthiest food, learn the best lessons possible, etc. If my kids came home from school to tell me about a problem they had, like a kid at the lunch table making fun of them, I would immediately start thinking they were being bullied and that I was going to have to move and find another school for them.

Marriage is another worry altogether. Since my parents were divorced, I always lived in fear of the same thing happening to me. I worried that my husband would find another woman better than me to make him happy. I worried that he would lose his job, we'd be out on the streets or have no money. Even when we didn't have any money and were literally living off of a single person student loan with five kids, I worried that we would never make it out of those trenches. It was like I lived in constant fear with no hope of things getting better (even when I really did have it good).

I've worried about friends, strangers, wars, rumors of war, my car breaking down, getting stuck in a storm, not being able to leave my house in the winter due to snow. I worried it wouldn't rain enough, then I'd worry it was raining too much. If my kids were minutes late on the bus, I imagined the bus turned over into some ditch, or worse yet, that they'd been kidnapped or encountered a mass shooter.

It didn't help that during those years my husband was obsessed with shows like, "Americas Most Wanted" or "Unsolved Mysteries" and real-life murder stories. It is a true wonder to me how I ever got any sleep. I would think about bad things all day and then fall asleep thinking about them. I lived in a constant and chronic worry mode and thought that it was solving my problems. I know a lot of my friends do/did the same thing.

I think that as women we have a tendency to take all the worries of the world onto our shoulders as if doing so will make them go away or become better. We want to protect our kids from any pain or struggle, even though doing so would prevent their personal growth and learning. The same thing goes for complaining (like I explained earlier in the book).

Somehow, we have gotten into some bad habits in our conversations. Bashing others, comparing, complaining, and worrying should be put behind us as we step into a new understanding of how blessed and capable we really are. We have a lot more to do with the things that happen to us than many of us really understand. When you read what I'm about to share, you too will understand the power that you wield.

We Are Like Magnets

Have you ever noticed on those days that you wake up and think, "This is going to be a terrible day," it is? If you are running late and rushing out the door because you'll never make it to your appointment or work on time, do you seem to get stuck behind the slowest drivers in the universe? When you think that you are going to have the best time of your life, do you? For me, that is almost always the case. It has always amazed me that we often experience self-fulfilling prophecies.

I never really understood why until I was introduced to the law of attraction. I learned that this law of the universe was as powerful as the law of gravity, probably even more so. It is working in every person's life all the time whether we know about it or not. It all starts with our thoughts.

At the root core of every single thing on this planet, we are all made up of the same exact thing: energy. That energy is always vibrating and there are as many frequencies on which it can vibrate as there are sands in the ocean. Each thought and feeling that we have determines what vibrational frequency we are on. Those frequencies then become like magnets, attracting things to us that are on the same frequency. This process determines what happens in our lives.

There are simple ways of describing this, such as: "What we think about expands" or "Where attention goes, energy flows." When we think about something long enough, we can make it a reality in our lives. Thought coupled with feeling is even more powerful. By feeling a strong emotion attached to a thought, we can immediately attract that thing into our lives.

Thus, worrying about something and having a strong feeling attached to that worry, not only does not help the situation, but can bring that bad thing right to us.

You see, the law of attraction doesn't bring us only the good things that we think about, but it attracts to us all the negative things that are on the same vibration as us as well. For example, I cannot possibly attract money into my life by travelling on the vibrational frequency of lack or feeling like I don't have enough of it. I cannot find true love when I truly believe or feel that I don't deserve it or can't find it. If I think that I'm not worthy or good enough, I will attract people into my life that will prove my limited belief to be true. If I worry that I am a bad mother, my children (or others) will find ways to make me feel even worse.

For this reason we need to cease all worry (at least as much as we can). We need to stop scaring our-selves to death. By thinking the worst-case scenario and feeling scared by it, we are actually attracting it into our lives like a moth to a flame. If we don't want to keep attracting things to worry about, we need to stop thinking and feeling them. When people try to tell me horror stories or share terrifying news about what is going on in the world, I try to cut them off as soon as I can. Filling my mind with negative things that I cannot control will not solve those things and will only attract more of them into my life. For that reason, my family got rid of cable a long time ago, and I now rarely read the newspaper. It is also why most of the wars on drugs/abortion/gangs, etc. don't really solve the problem, they just direct more energy towards those things. I wish I could tell all the news and media stations this, for I believe it would make a monumental difference in our world.

The same thing goes with telling our stories. How many people do you know are living in the past, always telling the same sad sob story about how something that happened 20 years ago ruined their entire lives or made them who they are today? Do you know someone that complains all the time and cannot seem to get over anything bad that happens to them? I wish that I could tell them what I know now. Every single time we repeat a story, good or bad, we dig it deeper into our subconscious and our real-time experiences. We are giving that story the power of how we feel in a new moment, in which that story need not exist. If we want to start having great stories to tell, we first need to stop repeating the bad ones. (Unless we are using them to help others out and show how we've overcome them.)

Complaining about things, living in the past, feeling like a victim, and making up excuses for how we feel NOW will only attract more things to us that we can complain, gripe, and worry about. It really is a law of the universe.

That being the case, we can control what comes to us by simply choosing to be happy now.

"When I look back on all these worries, I remember the story of the old man who said on his deathbed that he had had a lot of trouble in his life, most of which had never happened." **Winston Churchill**

Don't Worry, Be Happy

One of my absolute favorite songs ever is by Bobby McFerrin called *"Don't Worry Be Happy."*[70] I grew up with this song in the 90's and it has been a go-to for me when things get hard. It has a bit of a Jamaican feel to it and makes you want to dance and be carefree. The message of the song is pretty powerful but often overlooked. He talks about how even if we have no money to pay rent, are being taken to court, and have no place to sleep at night, we should be happy and stop worrying. When we worry, we double the problem.

I must have heard this song a million times in my lifetime, but until recently I never really paid attention to the lyrics (besides the name being repeated over and over). Have you ever done that before? Listened to a song and never really paid attention to what it was truly saying? I hate to admit it, but I have been guilty of such a thing many times. There have been songs that I loved as a teenager that will come on while I'm in the car with my kids and I feel like I need to change the station because I don't want my kids hearing those lyrics! Music can have a powerful effect on our minds and moods.

By learning to be happy *now*, regardless of the situation we are in or the horrific things that *could* happen, we can absolutely change our lives in an instant. Worrying is really just a way of focusing on our fears of what *could* happen rather than being engaged in what *is* happening.

It's one thing to say, "stop worrying about that" and another thing to actually be able to do it. So many of us are conditioned to seeing and imagining the worst that we don't know how to stop our worrying thoughts for more than a few seconds. Guess what? I've already taught you a few things that will help with that and have a few more up my sleeve!

How to Stop Worrying

Earlier in this book we talked about deep breathing and mindfulness. Both of these practices lead to a more peace-filled mind and the ability to let go of the thoughts and feelings that nag at us and plague our minds. Another thing I love to do is to meditate, but I will leave that subject for another book since deep breathing and mindfulness are sufficient for our needs here.

In addition to those tools, there are a few more that really help me when I have pressing worries on my mind or when the inner fear wants to bubble up. I like to imagine myself floating peacefully on a river or a pool, enjoying the clouds. Occasionally, even during our peaceful moments, we encounter harsh dark clouds that threaten our serenity. When those float into the picture in my mind, I see them and observe them as they quickly float on by without causing me the fear and dread they used to. I then replace them with good uplifting thoughts that make me feel better instantly.

I have also been learning how to increase my faith and diminish my fear. Worry is really just another form of fear, or lack of faith.

Learning to see things with an eye of faith rather than fear has liberated me from the panic, anxiety, and stress that I used to experience regularly. It has given me wings to fly rather than thinking I shouldn't try.

I know I mentioned the scripture about the lilies of the field earlier in this book, but I want to return to it for a moment, because it is powerful once we truly understand it. When we can get to the point where we feel like a lily in the field or a sparrow in the sky, not worrying about where our next meal is coming from or what the rest of the day, month, year of our life is going to be like, we know that we have achieved something spectacular. We are free. We achieve true faith. Where faith is, fear cannot be.

This means that when we have faith, or perfect trust that all things are always working out for our good, we no longer need to worry about anything. Faith is believing that things are going according to the plan of a higher power, one that has our infinite happiness and joy in mind. Faith is knowing that no matter what seemingly bad things happen in our lives, they happen for a reason. Learning to look for it, we can find the meaning behind any circumstance. If we can see them through a higher perspective, we can grow and become better. Some of the hardest trials of my life have formed me into the person I am today. Without them, I would not know what I know now and would not be who I am.

Have you ever heard anyone say (usually after a trial) that they are grateful that it happened? I sure have. Many of the most wise and inspiring people I know have risen from the ashes life gave them and become truly victorious. They have allowed their struggles, hardships, and temptations to become opportunities for transformation. They not only make lemonade out of the lemons life deals them, but lemon bars, lemon cake, pesto or garlic lemon sauce, poppyseed lemon muffins, etc. They know how to make many great things happen from something bitter. They squeeze the most out of sour situations.

When we have true faith, our worries take wings and fly out of our lives. We are able to face our fears and walk through them rather than run from them. We can do things afraid, knowing that somehow, they will make us stronger, more resilient, and empower our faith.

Writing this book has been a huge act of faith on my part. The ugly thoughts of my inner critic have popped up multiple times, nearly scaring me enough to stop writing and give up. I've feared failure and rejection and faced a lot of self-doubt.

However, I have learned that one of the best ways to overcome fear and strengthen my faith is to exit my comfort zone and do things afraid. Walking through fear and pursuing a dream (or happiness) *while afraid*, is showing true faith. One of my favorite mentors, Alison Prince, tells those of us in her class to "Kick fear in the teeth" or say, "Not today Satan, not today" when we are afraid.

I have enough faith in the things that I have shared in this book that I could not allow my fears to take over. I know deep down that some mother out there needed this book and will become a happier person and a better mother because of something in here. If all this book does is help one mother increase her joy, it will have all been worth it. *Even if that mother is me.*

The Bright Side or the Brown Side

When we start seeing through the lens of faith, we are in essence "looking on the bright side," or seeing the good in every situation.

I absolutely love the bright side. I love bright colors and find joy in light things. My favorite color has always been yellow, the brighter the better (just not neon). I always try to look on the bright side of every situation in my life and to find the good in it all. Even in my worrying days, things always seemed to work out in the end. Sometimes I couldn't see the "light" until years later, but like they say, "hindsight gives you 20/20 vision".

As humans we like to divide ourselves and compartmentalize who we are. We say we are optimists or pessimists, glass "half empty or half full" kind of people, or that things are black or white. I've been thinking about the extreme opposites we tend to use to find our differences and I've come to a realization that there is beauty in it all.

One morning, as I was meditating, it came to my mind that the natural opposite of "the bright side" would be the "dark side." However, as I lay there with eye mask on, basking in the serenity of the complete darkness of the early morning, I couldn't help but realize that I loved the darkness. So, I started trying to think of something that I didn't like as much as brightness or darkness. I thought about brown.

Most things that are brown are downright gross and ugly, upon first inspection. The first obvious thing that pops into my mind is poop. Yep, I'm writing about that nasty stuff that smells and makes our life stink, *again*. When you are a mother of 5, you see, smell, and clean poop on a regular basis and I could fill your mind with all sorts of nasty stories about it, but don't worry, I won't. I then thought about dirt. I have never been one to play in the mud or enjoy getting dirty, it is messy and hard to clean. Yep, feces and dirt were about the grossest most brown things that I could think of.

However, as I pondered on these two dirty and gross things, I realized that they were both very necessary ingredients for life. I started thinking about how I love putting manure in soil in the spring because it fertilizes my garden to the point where the vegetables and fruit grow really well. I considered how the very act of going number two allows our bodies to release unwanted toxins and things that we do not need. Being able to change diapers means that I have babies, and that means I have brought life to the world, and what a blessing that is!

I continued on this train of thought and gave thanks for the ability to go to the bathroom and that it was a sign our bodies were functioning properly and healthfully. Our feces can give us clues to our health and help us know if we are treating our bodies right. Without dirt, we could have no food to eat, for we couldn't plant seeds or have anything in which to grow things. Dirt forms the foundation of every flower and tree in the world. Without it, our lives would not have the beauty of roses, daffodils or lilacs. We would not have the needed oxygen to live and to breathe.

As I pondered about how much the "brown" things in life do for us, I became more and more fascinated by the idea that we need the stinky and dirty things in our lives. They give our lives flavor, fertilize our faith, and allow beauty to grow. They feed our souls the nutrients we need to appreciate the wonders of life. Without the bitter, we could never taste the sweet. Without the brown, we couldn't appreciate the bright.

So next time you are faced with the choice of "looking on the bright side" realize that in the end, everything is the bright side. Everything that happens to us is for our good. If we look for it, we can find the reason behind every crappy thing that happens and soon be grateful for it. There is only good, if we have the eyes and hearts to see it. That leads me to a very insightful dream experience I had.

The Dream That Woke Me Up

One day several years ago I woke up from a very powerful and scary dream. It was actually more of a recurring nightmare. I had this deep-rooted fear of losing one of my children, especially to them drowning. I don't really know where that insecurity came from, though as mothers we are constantly bombarded with things that threaten the safety and well-being of our children. It doesn't matter where it comes from as much as learning that it is there and how to get over it. Anyhow, I dreamed that my then youngest child (about five years old at the time) had drowned in the pond that my husband was adamant that we dig in our front yard. I was a nervous wreck about it.

My husband had dreamed of owning his own pond or lake for as long as I'd known him, but for years I fought him on it and said we could dig one only once all of our kids could swim. He was kind enough to hold off until such was the case. However, that didn't stop my worrying mind. Once I heard and saw the tractors tearing up our front yard to make the biggest pond I'd ever seen (it really is more of a small lake), my fears and worries took over. It seemed that every week I was having a dream about my kids drowning and it was terrifying. Many times, I would wake up in tears, not knowing what to do. I wanted to stop the digging. I wanted to live in fear and do all in my mama-bear power to protect my kids from the "evil" water and to make sure they survived.

This particular dream wasn't very different than the rest. My daughter drowned, it was my husbands' fault, and I was a basket case. It felt so real and so scary that I probably stopped breathing and definitely woke up crying. However, when I woke up I realized that the Lord had allowed me to face my deepest fear in a dream rather than in reality. He had given me the gift of experiencing deep and profound pain without having to truly experience it. I felt the anguish and bitterness of what would be the worst thing that could ever happen to me, but it only lasted for a few hours rather than for the rest of my life. I know that many mothers are not blessed with it being only a dream and I am so sorry for their loss. It truly is horrifying. It is not something I would wish on my worst enemy, not even a snake.

I began to ask myself some hard questions to get to the root of my fear. What was I so afraid of? Who would I be if I truly did lose a child? Did I really believe that I would see them again after this life? Did I have faith that the God I knew and loved was really looking after me and always allowing the things that are best for me to happen? For my children? Was I holding some kind of resentment against my husband, since the kids drowning was always his fault?

It dawned on me after this serious self-reflection, that I was living in fear and not faith. By allowing my mind to go down these terrible paths I was further able to diagnose my true problem. I allowed myself to think about what would truly be the worst thing that could happen. I imagined that if my daughter had died, she would be in a better place. Then I saw that although it would be extremely hard, I could get over the pain and use it to become a powerful teacher and healer. I could use my tragedy to lift and console others that had experienced such a loss.

I know a few mothers that have done just that- they have inspired and healed many through their example of moving forward after losing a child. One such mother lost her child suddenly to a strange undiagnosed sickness at the age of 8. The child's teacher and mother got together to create one of the most magical traditions our town has. Every November, right before the Christmas season, organizations, schools, and individuals start filling up our city park with memory trees for loved ones that have passed and for people to enjoy. They have an organization that lights up our park for the entire Christmas season, making it an even more magical time of year. It is straight out of a Hallmark movie scene and nothing short of spectacular, and it all came about because of the desire to remember and shine light in a dark place. Another friend wrote a book about overcoming the loss of her son and acts as a profound example of overcoming adversity and making the most out of extremely rough situations.

Anyhow, back to my dream. I learned that I didn't fully trust my husband. That I worried he did not care about the kids as much as I did, because he'd allow them to drown in his precious pond. These things were completely false and ridiculous. Of course, my husband loved me and our children. He would never intentionally hurt them or let them die if he could do anything in his power to prevent it.

The pond really wasn't something to fear. It could be a huge blessing for our family. My husband saw it as an opportunity to swim, fish, boat, and enjoy nature together as a family. My mind was changed after that powerful self-evaluation. For once, I was able to see the huge hole in my front yard as a blessing and not a curse. I was extremely grateful that I was able to learn these lessons from a recurring dream rather than a true living nightmare.

It has been a few years now since we dug the pond, and I admit that I love it. It has been a fun blessing for our family, for which I am grateful.

Since then, I have been able to replace most of my chronic worries with bright and motivating beliefs about a future I love. I have been able to change the words I use in my mind with more powerful and faith-filled vocabulary that ease my pain and enliven my soul. I have finally learned to think on the bright side, to see the glass full and able to be consistently filled rather than half empty, and I can see things with an eye of faith not fear.

Another one of my favorite songs has always been, "*I Can See Clearly Now*" by Johnny Nash[71]. After that dream and the lessons learned, I changed the end phrase to something that I hold dearer to my heart. I hope it can help you too, for I believe it with all my heart.

"I can see clearly now my faith is strong."

The famous line from "Amazing Grace" is similar: "Was blind but now I see."

When our faith becomes strong, our fears and worries become weak. Our problems become puzzles to be solved, and our failures become a pathway to where we long to be. We can see more clearly *why* certain things are put in our path.

There are no longer any obstacles in my way, but a perfect path of stepping stones and opportunities to grow to a higher perspective every day of my life. I know now that we can find meaning behind every single thing that happens in our lives. Sometimes the things that seem really bad or annoying are the things that we need to move on to the next level of learning and growth. It makes me smile.

What Makes You Smile?

Did you know that we can literally smile our worries away? Have you ever tried to smile when you are really mad or sad? I have learned that when I feel such emotions, if I can't get them out of my mind, I can smile them away. If you count down from five and tell yourself to smile by the time you get to one, then hold that smile for 10 seconds, you will immediately feel better. Try it the next time you feel bad. It seems physically impossible to think or feel badly when we are smiling. Science has also proven the power of a smile. Here are a few of the positive benefits that a simple smile can bring into our lives:

- **Smiling makes you more attractive.** The act of smiling makes you appear more confident and happy. The emotions associated with smiling trick our subconscious mind into thinking that we are happy even if we aren't- like the "fake it 'til you make it" philosophy. Confident and happy people are more attractive than angry, sad, or non-smiling people.
- **Smiling relieves stress.** When you are feeling overwhelmed or like you can't take it another minute, try smiling. It will lighten your load instantly.
- **Smiling elevates our mood.** It releases chemicals in our brain like dopamine and serotonin, that help us feel happier. It is like a natural anti-depressant.
- **Smiling is contagious.** Have you ever had a child come up to you with a huge smile on their face? I don't know about you, but when I see a child smile, I can't help but smile myself. When I see a friend, family member, or even strangers smile, I feel like smiling, too.
- **Smiling is actually good for your overall health as well.** It can boost your immune systems, lower your blood pressure, and make you feel good. If you are feeling sick or unhealthy, smile more and heal yourself.
- **Smiling makes you look younger, seem more successful and stay positive.**[72][73]

If that isn't enough, it just feels good to smile. I know when I have had a bad day or feel down, a simple smile from a perfect stranger can instantly lift me up. Kids are especially good at making me both smile and frown. Being a mother is seriously a roller-coaster of emotions. However, when we can learn to smile even amongst the spilled milk, dried snot, whiny voices, and crying, we can move mountains in our own homes and raise our children in an environment that helps them soar.

I love the little children's song, "If you chance to meet a frown[74], do not let it stay. Quickly turn it upside down and smile that frown away. No one likes a frowny face, change it for a smile. Make the world a better place by smiling all the while." What a simple yet profound message to share with our kids and to practice ourselves.

I'm sure you've heard the saying, "You're never fully dressed without a smile." Let's admit it, many of us stay-at-home mothers don't even get dressed during the day. I know I said this before, but as a young mother, I found that more often than not I would stay in my pajamas or my workout clothes until right before my husband came home. I had no one to impress and nowhere to go, so why get ready?

I'll tell you why. There is something psychologically fulfilling about putting our best foot forward and taking care of our bodies *for ourselves*. We feel more confident and ready to take on the day when we are fully dressed (including being showered and wearing our smile). We can happily open the door to any friends or neighbors who might pass by and know that we are presenting our best selves. Our children will see our example of taking care of our bodies and will want to do the same.

It's the same affect that making our bed can do for our rooms. When we see a bed made, it makes the entire room feel better. When we are fully ready for the day, we too feel better. You don't need to go all out with the makeup and hair, but if that is what makes you feel beautiful, then do it. Doing what makes us feel good about ourselves will always bring us more joy and make life more fun. If wearing your pajamas all day makes you feel happy and good about yourself, then by all means, do it! I sometimes do. Just don't forget, that no matter what you are wearing, you are not fully dressed without that beautiful smile that is uniquely yours.

I'm not saying that we need to walk around smiling 24/7, that would not be human. There will be days of sorrow, disappointment, hormonal outbursts, and unexpected surprises, and that is okay. Heck, there might even be long drawn out months or years of sadness or depression, and that is okay too. We need not beat ourselves up or feel "less than" for not feeling happy all the time. It is okay, and if we feel that way, we are not alone.

However, I doubt anyone likes that feeling and I bet that those suffering through depression would love to get out of it as soon as possible. If so, know that it is absolutely okay and beneficial to seek help. There is nothing to be ashamed of when it comes to doing what it takes to help us overcome our negative feelings. If that means taking some pills or talking it over with a professional, do it! Taking care of our well-being is one of the best things we, as mothers, can do for ourselves and our families.

We need to give ourselves a break and realize that nothing needs to be permanent, no matter how long it seems to linger. Being more mindful of how we are feeling and knowing that those emotions are temporary rather than permanent can make a massive difference in how we feel overall. The more mindful and compassionate we are with ourselves and our feelings, the more we will find ourselves wanting to smile.

In addition to smiling, another great thing to fight off our worries and lighten our moods is laughter.

I took my oldest out to pizza this week. She is three. When we got in the car to go home, she said, "Mama, today was a special day. You took me to get pizza. I'm in pizza happiness." Story shared by a Facebook Friend

---

Laughter Is the Best Medicine

Laughter has many of the same benefits as smiling. You know the saying, "laughter is the best medicine"? Well, that is a scientifically proven fact. While researching the benefits of laughter, I found that it aids our lives in the same ways as smiling, but maybe in an even more powerful way. [75]

I have even read about people curing themselves from cancer by watching funny movies non-stop.

Have you seen the laughing video that went viral about a year ago? It took place on a subway or train of some sort. It began with people sitting there minding their own business or reading the paper. Then someone gets on the train and starts laughing uncontrollably. Soon their laugh becomes contagious and the people around them start laughing. By the end of the video the entire train is laughing, even long after the originator of the laugh has gotten off. As a viewer I couldn't help but laugh as well. You can literally brighten up an entire train or room full of people by making them laugh. Innocent and simple humor is the best. Laughing at the expense of others does not bring the same kind of benefits or fulfillment.

We can lighten the mood in our homes by sharing a good laugh. When things get tense and out of control, it can be a great thing to let down your guard as a mother and do something ridiculous and silly enough to evoke laughter from your family. My mom used to get out the broom and cackle like a witch when we started fighting. She'd even occasionally threaten us with her gas if she felt especially silly. It did the trick and lightened the mood of the home every time. I'll occasionally start talking in crazy accents and it always gets my kids' attention. Don't worry if you aren't naturally funny or creative in this way. Doing something completely out of your normal character you'll get your kids attention and make everyone smile if not laugh.

When you feel yourself start to worry, look up a funny video where other people are laughing, and you'll feel better in no time. You can also use music to brighten your mood. Make a playlist of songs that make you feel good and play them when you need a pick-me-up. I have playlists of happy songs, songs that remind me of a particularly good time in my life, and songs that make me want to get up and dance. Music, smiles, and laughter take our minds off the things that could happen and help us focus on things that bring joy *now*.

Another simple thing you can do to feel happy is to write a happy or fun list. Take out a piece of paper and start writing down as many things as you can think of that make you smile or feel happy. Make a point to do/see/watch something from your list every single day.

Let's all try to make our lives and the world a happier place by smiling and laughing all the while. Let's try to stop taking life so seriously and bend the rules and rigidity a bit. When we get dressed in the morning, let us remember that life is meant to be enjoyed. Joy is in the journey, not in worrying about where the journey might end up. When we get a flat tire or run out of gas, instead of blowing up with extreme worry or fear, why not choose to see the bright side? Why not choose to laugh it off and find the meaning in the unforeseen events?

It takes less than a second to smile but can improve your entire day. It can make you happy now, and the happier we are, the higher the energetic frequency we travel on. The higher our vibrational frequency, the better our lives will be. We will find more fun and happy things in life that are attracted to us. It's not just me, or your mom saying this stuff anymore, it is proven to be true through science.

Let's make it a point to find things every day that make us smile, laugh, and feel good. Life is too short to be worried all the time. We don't have to wait until we are retired, our kids are grown and more responsible, or our trials are all gone to feel good. Those days might never come. We can choose happiness and joy at any given moment of any given day if we want to. The power is always ours and can become a way of life if we practice it long enough.

I choose joy. How about you?

Sunday school teacher: Tell me, Johnny. Do you say prayers before eating?

Johnny: No, ma'am, I don't have to. My mom's a good cook.

Chapter Highlights:

- I used to have a terrible addiction to worrying. I thought that worrying about something or imagining the worst-case scenario of a situation meant that I could somehow feel better about it or solve it. Has worrying ever solved your problems?

- I think that as women we have a tendency to take all the worries of the world onto our shoulders as if doing so will make them go away or become better. We want to protect our kids from any pain or struggle, even though doing so would prevent their personal growth and learning.

- The law of attraction is as powerful as the law of gravity, probably even more so. It is working in every person's life all the time whether we know about it or not.

- We are all like magnets. At the root core of every single thing on this planet, we are all made up of the same exact thing: energy. That energy is always vibrating and there are as many frequencies on which it can vibrate as there are sands in the ocean.

- "What we think about expands" or "Where thoughts go energy flows." When we think about something long enough, we can make it a reality in our lives.

- We need to cease all worry. We need to stop scaring ourselves to death. By thinking the worst-case scenario and feeling scared by it, we are actually attracting it into our lives like a moth to a flame.

- Complaining about things, living in the past, feeling like a victim, and making up excuses for how we feel NOW will only attract more things to us that we can complain, gripe, and worry about.

- By learning to be happy now, regardless of the situation we are in or the horrific things that *could* happen, we can absolutely change our lives in an instant. Worrying is really just a way of focusing on our fears of what *could* happen rather than being engaged in what *is* happening.
- Learning to see things with an eye of faith rather than fear can free you from panic and worry.
- Where faith is, fear cannot be.
- Next time you are faced with the choice of "looking on the bright side" realize that in the end, everything is the bright side. Everything that happens to us is for our good. Writing a simple list of that make you smile or feel happy can increase your happiness.
- Sometimes the things that seem really bad or annoying are the things that we need to move on to the next level of learning and growth.
- We can literally smile and laugh our worries away.

Actions to Take:

1. Reflect on your own personal worries. Are you a chronic worrier? What action steps can you take to stop worrying and start fortifying your faith today?

_____

_____

_____

2. Pay attention to what you think about the most. Try to think about the things that you really want and how to achieve them rather than focusing on the things you lack.

3. What do you complain about, and how can you change that into a better habit?

_____

_____

_____

4. What makes you smile or laugh? Download some funny jokes, videos, memes, and playlists for when you need to change your vibration.

5. Write a list of things that make you happy, that bring a smile to your face, or that you think are fun. Look at the list whenever you want to feel good.

6. Place your hand on your heart and repeat out loud, "My smile can change lives. I have a beautiful smile." (then smile).

CONCLUSION

"You'll never change your life until you change something you do daily. The secret of your success is found in your daily routine."
—John C. Maxwell

"Most psychologists agree that fully 95 percent of everything you think, feel, and do will be determined by your habits... all habits are learned and therefore learnable."
—Brian Tracy

I can't believe we are already here at the end of the book. Congratulations to you for making it this far. According to Alex Becker, in *The 10 Pillars of Wealth*, 90 percent of the people who start a book don't finish it[76], so you, my friend, are spectacular. I hope that you have been putting into action the simple things to help you find joy in motherhood and life.

Every little habit that has been covered in this book is fast, free, and makes life more fun. Sometimes we have a tendency to underestimate the small and simple things of life. Like the power of a smile to bring joy to another, or the smell of a rose, or the ability to breathe. However, when we learn to become more mindful of all the amazing things this world has to offer, we begin to notice the huge difference small things make.

I remember being floored by how my life took a complete 180 after my first baby was born. How could something or someone so small make such a huge impact on my heart and my time? It was amazing to me that someone less than ten pounds and one second old could hold my entire heart. It was alarming how that same someone could require me to sacrifice so much time around the clock to meet their needs and respond to their beck and call. Motherhood is not for the faint of heart. It is a calling and a blessing. It makes women out of girls and can often make us feel like somewhat of a failure.

The tiny little life-hacks that I have both scientifically and personally explained in this book can absolutely alter your life in a matter of days, if not minutes. They will yield instant results and bring you peace, joy, and hope. Please do not underestimate the power of the seemingly small and insignificant things in life.

My driveway always reminds me of such a thing. It is long, unpaved, and covered in gravel. At least once a year we have to have it graded so as to make the bumps and lumps become smooth and drivable again. We live in a place where it rains a lot. When the rain sprinkles and only comes down on occasion, it is hardly even noticeable on the driveway. However, when it continues to rain for hours on end or even days or weeks, it takes a huge toll really fast. Over time, constant and relentless tiny drops of rain make a giant rivet in the gravel, where a flood of water can easily travel down our hill. Water has been known over time to turn mountains to valleys and river rock to slate. It has amazing power when it is allowed to continuously pour drop by drop onto any surface.

Our daily habits can make the same difference in our lives. By applying mindfulness and deep breathing, walking in nature, changing your words, repeating affirmations, giving compliments, setting scary goals, hydrating your body, smiling, and getting quality sleep you will absolutely see massive results in a very short amount of time. The most important things that produce the longest, far-reaching results fast are to develop gratitude, the ability to stop worrying, and live with an eye of faith. Drop by drop, each habit will pave your way to happiness and peace and allow you to make the most of the journey of life. You will become a master experimenter in the kitchen of life, always learning new ways to be happy for the lemons life gives you and making the most amazing things from them.

Best of all, you will become the kind of mom you always wanted to be. You will be full of unconditional love, endless reservoirs of patience and compassion and energy. Does that mean that you won't have bad days and will never feel worry, guilt, or like a failure again? Absolutely not. However, you will be more mindful and aware of how you are feeling and be able to nip it in the bud before it has a long-lasting negative effect on yourself and your family.

Your children will always adore you, but raising them with mindfulness and contentment will prevent them from having the issues that the majority of adults struggle with today. Taking the time to take care of you will be the best thing you ever do for yourself or your kids.

Let me give you one more piece of math before you go, so you can recognize how little these techniques are asking of you. If you were to take ten minutes a day to practice even a few of these habits, do you know how much time that would be in a year? It equals roughly two and a half days. With 365 days in a year, taking the equivalent of less than three of them to make life-improving and long-lasting changes is absolutely something you can do. No matter how many little ones you have pulling on your leg or keeping you up at night, it is more than possible to find more than a measly two and half days a year or ten minutes a day to find joy.

If, however, you wanted to *massively* improve your life and do every single habit to the fullest on a daily basis, let me assure you that it wouldn't take as much time as you think. If you were to take just ten percent of your time doing all ten of these habits, it would be roughly an hour and a half a day. I get all of that done in the wee hours of the morning. If you did that every day for a week, it would be the equivalent of ten and a half hours. If you were to keep that up for a year, it would equal 546 hours, or almost 23 days. That is less than a month's worth of time out of a year, and is about six percent of your year. Does that make it seem doable? I sure hope so.

I like charts and having a review at the end of a book. For that reason, I have made the following recap of this book, so you can remember all of the little things that can add up to an amazing life. I want you to see how easy it can be to put yourself first and find time to feel refreshed and experience the joys of motherhood and of becoming our best selves.

Habit	Time Commitment
1. Gratitude Journal Wake up and appreciate things Little black book	5 minutes 1 minute 1 minute
2. Be Mindful Deep Breathe Self-reflection of stress	1 minute 5 minutes (minimum) 1 minute
3. Nature Walk Drink water/Stay Hydrated	10 minutes 1 minute or less
4. Give a compliment to yourself Compliment someone else	30 seconds 30 seconds
5. Change your words	Daily awareness, no time
6. Mirror Work Affirmations Set your day up for success	5 seconds 1 minute 1 minute
7. Get enough sleep Lull yourself to sleep (hypnosis, etc.)	8-10 hours Add it to your night's sleep
8. Visualize your dream life Write/read your future document Find your why/review it daily	5 minutes 5 minutes 1 minute
9. Set Goals/work on them Celebrate the small things Exercise *Magical mornings	5 minutes+ 1 minute 4 minutes minimum 1 1/2 hours* for the overachiever who wants to get everything done before the kids get up
10. Look on the bright side Get dressed/showered Smile/laugh	1 second or more- a shift in mindset Few minutes 1 second/minutes
Total time: Bare minimum (if you did all the habits) If you did the magical morning/evening and got all the habits in at once	Around 45-50 minutes 1 ½ hours or less

As you can tell, these are estimates, and you can give or take a few minutes here and there and customize these habits to your lifestyle. Try to make it easy on yourself. Start with one habit, then add another one once you have mastered it. In no time at all, you will find that adding these little things to your life will make you happier, healthier, and feeling more confident as a mother and as a woman. Ten minutes (or less) is all it takes to feel a lot less stress and more joy. Everyone has ten minutes, even the busiest moms I know. It is how we prioritize those minutes that counts.

I hope by now, you believe that achieving the impossible is possible. I hope this book has left you feeling refreshed and ready to go and tackle the world (or at least the laundry). I pray that you feel excited and have desires to "be selfish" and put yourself first for at least one percent of your day. I have a dream that each and every mother out there will not only know of her worth and value but feel it deep within her soul. That we can all appreciate how needed we are and know that our children consider us precious and priceless and irreplaceable. And if they feel that way about us, so can we.

Every mother I know is busy, but there are ways to turn the mundane into the magical in very little time.

I hope someday to personally meet you, to fill you with love and light and to encourage you to reach for the moon. You are incredible. Thanks for taking this journey with me.

May your days be full of smiles and laughter, that you become worry-free and super happy!

If you have enjoyed this book and journey, would you do me a small favor? Would you please take one minute, right now, to review it on Amazon? The more people that review, the more Amazon will show this book too. Thanks in advance, I appreciate you!

Lastly, always remember that YOU ARE MORE THAN ENOUGH, AND YOU ARE LOVED!

WANT HELP APPLYING WHAT YOU'VE LEARNED?

I know that it is hard enough to read a book, let alone do what it tells you to do.

However, that is where the magic is.

If we do not apply the things we learn, then they are not going to impact our lives or transform us in any way. Reading becomes merely something to amuse us for a short while, then be forgotten.

I have promised you throughout this book that by applying even a few of the habits into your life, you will find less stress and more joy. I want that for you! Do you?

If you are ready to make the change, I have an invitation for you!

My husband and I have created challenge courses, home study programs, and coaching opportunities to help you take your life to the next level. Change is so much easier to embrace when we have other people helping and cheering us on.

You can find out more on our websites and blogs:

www.chooseanamazinglife.com or
www.refreshformoms.com

You can also email me with any questions at:
nichole@chooseanamazinglife.com or
nichole@refreshformoms.com

I would love to have you join me on my Facebook group and help you make the impact you were born to in this world! I can't wait to hear from you and get to know you!

All my love,

Nichole

ACKNOWLEDGEMENTS

This book would not have been possible without the support and aid of many people. I'd like to express my appreciation and gratitude to them for helping me make my dreams come true...

First, to my husband and best friend, Nathan. Thank you for being my number one cheerleader, for believing in me even when I didn't, and for supporting me through this entire process. I am so glad that we chose each other and that I get to raise our kids and experience life with you.

To my six beautiful children, I am such a better person because of you. You have taught me more in our years together than I could possibly express in one book. You are my world and I love being your mother. Thank you for giving me the stories and experiences necessary to make this book happen!

To my mother, you are one of my best friends. I love you dearly and appreciate all you have done, do, and will do to help me grow and become who God intended me to be.

To my father, who although no longer with us, continues to teach and inspire me. Thank you for your love and support throughout my life.

To all my friends and family that supported me and encouraged me throughout the writing and transforming process, thank you from the bottom of my heart. I appreciate you taking the time to help me edit, proof-read, find fun and joy on the journey, and teaching me hard lessons.

To those that helped make this book a reality and coached me through the process: Kary Oberbrunner & the AAE tribe, my partner Dana Lyons, and my designers, Sara Ometo and Tracy VanHolder, thank you!

To those that have helped me grow by teaching me hard lessons, labeling me, criticizing me, and allowing me to learn things that I couldn't have any other way, I thank you from the places in my heart only forgiveness and true love can penetrate. You have transformed me into who I am today, and I wouldn't be the same without you. Thanks for the tough love!

Last, but certainly not least, I owe everything I am to the father of my soul, my creator, my everything. I feel so grateful for the connection and love I feel from on high and for the opportunity to be an instrument for Him.

DEDICATION TO MY DAD

The last text I ever got from my dad has a similar theme to what I have written about. I share it here, so that his legacy can be passed on as well:

> "No matter how hard you think your life might be now, and no matter how hard you expect and prepare for a happy, slower, less stressful future- don't count on it. Sometimes the pressure cooker of life gets hotter and hotter and under more and more pressure the older we get. So, enjoy life NOW my sweet daughter! With all it's ups and downs, positive's and negatives, it's still a beautiful ride with more twists and turns than we could ever understand viewing it from pre-mortal heaven. So, enjoy and savor every experience- good or bad, pleasant or painful... that's why we're here! And some day, all will be well."

—Stephen Lew Cook

REFERENCES

1 Ramis, Harold and Rubin, Danny. (1993) Ground Hog Day. United States

2 https://greatergood.berkeley.edu/article/item/how-gratitude-changes-you-and-yourbrain; psychologytoday.AmyMorin:7scientifically-provenbenefitsofgratitude.

3 dictionary.com definition of gratitude

4 *The New Testament KJV Luke 17 vs. 12-18*

5 Dispenza, Joe. *You are the Placebo*. Hay House Inc. 2014 p.14

6 Byrne, Rhonda. *The Power. Atria* Publishing Group. 2010 p. 136

7 Annalee Skarin: *Ye are Gods*. The Philosophical Library. *1952* p. 97

8 Frankl, Viktor. *Mans' Search for Meaning*. Beacon Press P. 86

9 http://happierhuman.com/benefits-of-gratitude.

10 Hardy, Darren. *The Compound Effect*. Da Capo Press. 2010 p.27

[11]   Walt Disney Productions. (1960) *Pollyanna*. United States

[12]   https://www.webmd.com/balance/stress.../ stress-symptoms-effects_of-stress-on-the-body

[13]   Lipton, Bruce. The Biology of Belief Hay House Inc. 2005

[14]   McGonigal, Kelly. *The Upside of Stress*. Avery an Imprint of Penguin Random House. 2016 p.28

[15]   MGM Studios, *Overboard*. (1987) United States

[16]   http://www.onepowerfulword.com/2010/1 0/18-benefits-of-deep-breathing-and-how.html

[17]   https://www.consciouslifestylemag.com/ benefits-of-breathing-deeply/

[18]   Jampolsky, Gerald G. and Cirincione Diane V. *Change Your Mind Change Your Life*. Bantam Books. 1993. P.87

[19]   https://www.activebeat.com/ your-health/6-ways-sun-exposur e-can-brighten-your-health/5/)

[20]   https://www.healthline.com/health/depression/ benefits-sunlight#mental-health

[21]   Fereydoon Batmanghelidj, M.D.: *Water Cures: Drugs Kill: How Water Cured Incurable Diseases*. Global Health Solutions. 2003

[22]   https:.//www.naturalnews.com/055200_water_ hydration_disease_prevention.html

[23]   Meyerowitz, Steve. *Water: The Ultimate Cure* Pilgrims Publishing. 2001

24 https://www.naturalnews.com/055200_water_ hydration_disease_prevention.html#

25 https://www.hsph.harvard.edu/nutritionsource/ healthy-drinks/sugary-drinks/

26 https://www.hsph.harvard.edu/nutritionsource/ healthy-drinks/sugary-drinks/

27 https://www.livestrong.com/article/41 2167-how-much-weight-will-you-lose-i f-you-drink-water-for-a-week/ Sara Tomm

28 https:.//www.naturalnews.com/055200_ water_hydration_disease_prevention.html# by Samantha Debbie

29 https://www.livestrong.com/article/41 2167-how-much-weight-will-you-lose-i f-you-drink-water-for-a-week/ Sara Tomm

30 Feature Films for Families. *Rigoletto, The Curse* (1993) United States

31 http://amplifyyourvoice.org

32 www.nationaleatingdisorders.org

33 www.eatingdisordershelp.com

34 Chapman, Gary. *The Five Love Languages.* Manjul Pub. 2010

35 https://www.goodreads.com/author/ quotes/16366094.Lauren_Jauregui

36 https://www.lifehack.org/articles/commu- nication/7-reasons-why-you-should-pay-co mpliment-someone-every-day.html

37 *New Testament: Hebrews Chapter 4 KJV vs. 12*

38   Dispenza, Joe. *You are the Placebo.* Hay House Inc. 2014 *p.71*

39   Dr. Emoto http://www.masaru-emoto.net/english/water-crystal.html

40   Robbins, Tony. *Awaken the Giant Within* Free Press. 1991 pgs. 202-207

41   YouTube Mindvalley, *The Biggest Disease Affecting Humanity: "I'm Not Enough"* by Marisa Peer

42   Dispenza, Joe. *You are the Placebo.* Hay House Inc. 2014 *p.75*

43   New Testament KJV Matthew 5:48

44   James Strong: *The New Strong's Expanded Exhaustive Concordance of the Bible*

45   James Strong: *The New Strong's Expanded Exhaustive Concordance of the Bible* p. 266

46   Hay, Louise. *Mirror Work* Hay House Inc. 2016

47   Tracy, Brian. *Million Dollar Habits* .Entrepreneur Press. 2017 p.28

48   YouTube Mindvalley, *The Biggest Disease Affecting Humanity: "I'm Not Enough"* by Marisa Peer

49   *New Testament Luke 15 KJV The Prodigal Son vs. 11-32*

50   Lipton, Bruce. *The Biology of Belief* Hay House Inc. 2005

51   National Sleep Foundation- https://sleepfoundation.org/sleep-news/do-women-need-more-sleep-men

52   https://www.healthline.com/health/
sleep-deprivation/effects-on-body#1

53   https://www.sleepassociation.org/about-sleep/
sleep-statistics; https://nutrition.org/
obesity-linked-sleep-deprivation.

54   https://www.sleepassociation.org/about-sleep/
sleep-statistics

55   www.comscore.com the 2017 U.S. Mobile App
Report

56   theatlantic.com/whendidtvwatchingpeak May
30, 2018).

57   Proctor, Bob. *Paradigm Shift* https://www.you-
tube.com/watch?v=z2IEiYM_iYM

58   Dispenza, Joe. Week Long Advanced Retreat.
Cancun Mexico June 2018

59   https://www.forbes.com/sites/annabelac-
ton/2017/11/03/how-to-set-goals-and-wh
y-you-should-do-it/#3F13B69A162D

60   Schwartz, David. *The Magic of Thinking Big
Prentice-Hall Inc.* 1959. p.204

61   http://www.goalband.co.uk/
goal-achievement-facts.html

62   https://www.inc.com/marcel-schwantes/science

63   forbes.com *Just 8% of People Achieve Their New Year's
Resolutions. Here's How They Do It.* Jan 1, 2013

64   Hill, Napoleon. *Think and Grow Rich (Sound Wis-
dom 2016) as quoted in Million Dollar Habits by
Tracy, Brian. Entrepreneur Press. 2017 p.25*

65   https://www.health.harvard.edu/
     newsletter_article/The_quickie_workout

66   http://julliengordon.com/
     jim-carrey-graduation-speech-transcript-maharish
     i-university-2014

67   https://www.goodreads.com/quotes/47721-nothi
     ng-has-a-stronger-influence-psychologically-on-th
     eir-environment-and

68   Alex Becker The 10 Pillars of Wealth. Brown
     Books Publishing Group. 2016. P. 19

69   https://www.goodreads.com/quo
     tes/884712-the-graveyard-is-the
     -richest-place-on-earth-because-it

70   Nicholson, William. 2017. Breathe. Brazil

71   McFerrin, Bobby. Simples Pleasures Album. Don't
     Worry Be Happy. 1988

72   Nash, Johnny. I Can See Clearly Now Album. I Can
     See Clearly Now. 1972

73   https://www.verywellmind.com/
     top-reasons-to-smile-every-day-2223755

74   https://www.verywellmind.com/
     top-reasons-to-smile-every-day-2223755

75   https://www.lds.org/music/library/
     childrens-songbook/smiles word by Daniel Tay-
     lor 1989

76   https://www.cancercenter.com/treatments/
     laughter-therapy/

77   Alex Becker *The 10 Pillars of Wealth* Brown Books
     Publishing Group. 2016. P. 165